Dylife

The industrial and social history
of a famous Welsh lead mine

To

Jim and Karon

Best Wishes

Michael

Dylife

The industrial and social history
of a famous Welsh lead mine

Michael Brown

ISBN: 0 86243 775 X

Printed and published in Wales
by Y Lolfa Cyf., Talybont, Ceredigion SY24 5AP
e-mail ylolfa@ylolfa.com
website www.ylolfa.com
tel. (01970) 832 304
fax 832 782

Contents

I am looking over the windswept hills,
But looking I am in vain,
For a glimpse of the place where I was born,
And it makes me weary with pain,
I shall never go back again to live,
Only for the last long rest,
Whatever time is left for me,
Dylife will always be best.

WILLIAM MORRIS RICHARDS
1899–1976

INTRODUCTION

There are many old lead mines and workings scattered across the mountains and valleys of mid Wales but probably none is as familiar to the industrial archaeologist as Dylife. Situated on the northern side of what has come to be known as the Central Wales Orefield, the lonely hills we tread here have long been inhabited. Indeed, Owen Hughes of Bugeilyn discovered flint arrowheads in the peat there, and we know the Romans were busy here at the time of their occupation.

It is important to remember that, prior to the 1800s, the name Dylife applied to the workings by the old coach road on the top of Dylife Hill, and that both Esgairgaled and Llechwedd Ddu were being worked as separate concerns. It was not until the early 1800s that the name Dylife encompassed all three workings. It was at this point that the method of company mining really started to eclipse the smaller type of operation that was previously so common. The reason for this eclipse can probably be attributed to several factors. The foremost of which was that Britain was becoming a far wealthier country, and people with money were more available to invest in such concerns. The repeal of the Mines Royal Act in 1693 gave the right to every landowner to develop and profit from any mineral resources on his property, regardless of their content, and probably went far in aiding the industry as a whole to expand. Also of importance were the various technical advancements made over the years. In 1692, gunpowder for blasting replaced the older, much slower method of fire setting, whilst such developments as the use of the steam engine for deep drainage also promoted expansion within the industry.

For nearly 100 years the Welsh lead industry boomed; between 1853 to 1877, the price of lead averaged over £21 a ton, but this was not to last, and towards the end of the century things went from bad to worse. In 1878 the average price of lead fell to £16 a ton and it had fallen to £9.5s a ton by 1894.

The home demand for lead was being met by the import of produce from Spain and, later, Australia and the USA. The resulting drop in home prices, the high level of royalties and the lack of capital due to a loss of faith in the home industry reduced the Welsh lead industry to a state from which, sadly, it would never recover.

I have spent many happy times at Dylife, both above and below ground, and find myself returning there time and time again, if for no other reason than just to sit on the hill and ponder over a forgotten world of candlelight and blasting powder.

For those with a deep interest in the old lead mines of mid Wales, although sadly out of print, David Bick's series of books, *The Old Metal Mines of Mid Wales,* cannot be praised too highly for providing a fascinating insight into the industrial history of the area.

MICHAEL BROWN
Belan, Pennant

1. Dylife – an Industrial History

Dylife lies in the north-west of Montgomeryshire, within five miles of the Cardiganshire boundary, at a height of nearly 1200 feet above sea level. Mining here did not really begin in earnest until the 1800s, although it is evident that Dylife was busy long before this period.

The late Rev. D Lloyd Jones of Llandinam, who was an authority on Roman history, related that the Romans worked Dylife as well as nearby Dyfngwm and that they had a furnace to smelt the ore on the north side of Llechwedd Ddu, just below the Star Inn, and from there they carried it to their fortress at Caersws. They had a fort on the top of Pen Dylife, at the place known as Pen y Crogbren; this was probably built to safeguard their interests in their mining activities. It is also said that the old miners had seen levels which they thought the Romans had cut. I heard a story of a wooden wheelbarrow, attributed to the Romans, being found at Dyfngwm; it crumbled to dust when exposed to the air. The level is half way up the upper part of the Clywedog Valley and can still be explored, with care. A coffin level 150 fathoms in length was also discovered in 1857, although its whereabouts today are a mystery; it is quite likely, however, that it was on the Dylife lode, somewhere in the vicinity of Pen Dylife. David Bick records that, in 1971, two men, Jon Savage and Tony Jarrat, came across just such a level some 75 feet down a shaft near Pen y Crogbren, although it had later been widened by blasting.

Since the time of the Roman occupation, the earliest reference I have been able to find with regard to Dylife is in the early 1600s, when two brothers, Mathew and Jose de Quester took over a lease '…of all mines of lead called Nant y Moynedeleaven otherwise Dolyoe, Bulch, Keylan and Robindor all within the Lordship of Cyfeilog' from a John Edisbury. In 1641, Thomas Bushell took over the Quester leases of Dylife and Bwlch Ceulan from Ann de Quester, widow of one of the former lessees. Little more is known about this period until 1691, when William Waller, before becoming Manager of the famous Company of Mine Adventurers, had visited Dylife and found it worthy to note, '…there they had shafts 50 or 60 yards deep.' Output was very low and the mine had to buy in ore to supplement its own output; also, problems frequently arose with flooding. In 1707, William Waller wrote to Sir Humphrey Mackworth:

> …as to Mr Harley's mine (Esgairgaled) it is above 20 yards under water and no level can be had to it … I am told that Mr Peck will throw up Mr Pugh's liberty (Pen Dylife) for work is now above 30 yards that they draw water under level and the water charge goes with the profit of both Mr Harley's and his. We had Mr Harley's ore at £3-10-00 per ton delivered at the mill and it cost him above £6 per ton. These things will not do without other management, and a level to each must be brought.

At this time, while Esgairgaled was being run by a Mr Edward Harley, the Esgairgaled shaft was sunk vertically about 15 yards north of the Esgairgaled lode to a depth of about 40 fathoms; the lode was about 18 yards wide and very hard. There is some reference to potter's ore being raised at Pen Dylife by a Mr Peck and a William Pugh. I believe the mine stayed in the same hands

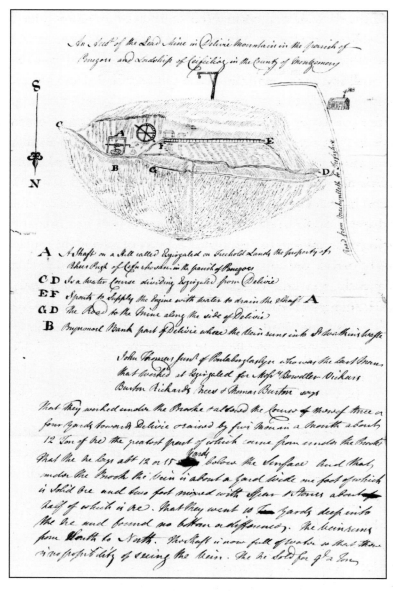

An early plan of workings at Esgairgaled, 1774. (N.L.W.)

until the early 1700s. From 1785 to 1800, the recorded history of Dylife is very vague; however, the research of David Bick has gone along way to throwing more light on this period. In 1785, a Mr Smedley was showing an interest in Esgairgaled and had plans to drive a level at Pencerrig, although, by 1787, both mines were being worked by separate companies. The Pencerrig Company included Miss Craven, Mrs Hughes and Sir Watkin's mineral agent, William Sawyer. At Esgairgaled there were a waterwheel and pumps, quite possibly the same wheel as featured in the 1774 plan. This machinery, which drained both mines, became a subject of dispute in 1788. There was talk by the Pencerrig Company of leasing their bottoms to Esgairgaled as a way of solving the problem. The boundary was also in dispute, as the stream, which divided the two works, had shifted course six to ten yards. Although Pencerrig was making good returns, it is said that the cost of carting the ore to the Dyfi consumed much of the profits. In 1788, William Sawyer, who had moved to Llanidloes, was proposing to bring in colliers, who, in his opinion, did twice the work of the lead men. In March 1791, the mine manager, Thomas Burton, complained that, 'I can get no bodey to take Llegwith Dee or Delivy as the price of ore is so low.' This is the earliest reference to Llechwedd Ddu and was discovered by David Bick. In 1793, all ore from Pencerrig, Esgairgaled and Dyfngwm was being sent to Georges of Bristol, with 96 tons being sent between May 1795 and May 1797, with 250 tons being held back due to the poor price of lead. By 1798 no work was being carried out at Pencerrig, Dylife or Llechwedd Ddu. Llechwedd Ddu was at work in 1808, when a winze sunk on the lode itself cut 3' 6" of solid lead at a depth of about 12 fathoms below the adit. The ore only extended for about 6 feet,

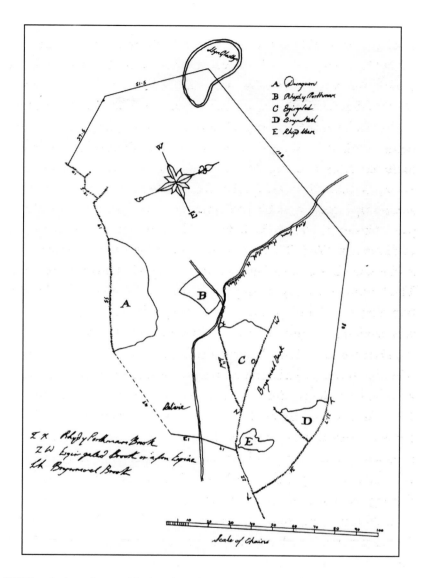

'1776 – A plan of part of Delivie Mountain to be leased to a Bagot Reade'.
Of utmost interest is the level marked on the south side of the Rhyd y Porthman
Brook. This is the earliest illustrated evidence of mining in the Llechwedd Ddu
area

Craig y Don, Aberdyfi

but by following this bunch the miners were led to a great body of ore that later led to the Llechwedd Ddu shaft being sunk.

Around this time, the cost of raising the water and stuff from Llechwedd Ddu proved to be too expensive, and the decision was made to drive a cross cut from the north side of Dylife hill, with the intention of meeting the Dyfngwm/Dylife lode. This cross cut became known as The Great Dylife Adit, and is about a third of a mile in length. It is worthy of note that the impressive entrance by the Llechwedd Ddu engine shaft was not the original means of access to the cross cut; the original entrance lay someway to the east, and was via an adit on the lode, still partially visible today in the form of a flooded pool. The new and larger entrance with inclined plane was added sometime later, to provide a more convenient means of access; the cross cut itself being large enough

Esgairgaled Area, 1840s, by David Bick. Note horse whim and tunnel for stream, the 37 ft wheel, and flatrods to Llewchwedd Ddu

to admit horses for pulling the trams.

In 1809, a Mr John Pugh of Aberdyfi joined forces with Hugh Williams, a timber merchant from Machynlleth. Hugh Williams had already worked the Dylife lode to the south of the old coach road, in partnership with a John Owen of Machynlleth. 22 tons of ore were to be produced this year. In 1811, three cargoes totalling 50 tons were sold to potters in Barnstaple and Bideford, on the north Devon coast (C. J. Williams).

In 1812, with prospects looking good, believing they could work the mine profitably, Williams and Pugh applied for a lease, although, by September of 1813, the lease remained unsigned as accounts between the lesser and lessee had not been agreed. By October of that year, the accounts had at last been prepared and submitted to the Agent for the Wynnstay Estate, William P Richards. These showed that a total of 293 tons of ore had been produced in the period 1809 – 1813. In 1812 steel grained ore was selling for £14 - £16 per ton and the potter's ore from £18 – 20 per ton. Whilst this was a fair price, the cost of carriage to Derwenlas in 1813 was high: a shilling per mile per ton, eroding profits considerably. The ore was shipped from here to smelters in Bristol, Flintshire and Liverpool.

Eventually, in 1814, the lease was signed for a period of 31 years; but by 1815 it was under threat of termination, unless articles of partnership were drawn up. They were never to appear. 38 tons of ore were raised in 1814 and 104 in 1815.

In the *Welsh History Review*, a very interesting article by C. J. Williams records that the partners were always slow to produce their accounts, and that in the 30-odd years during which Williams and Pugh ran the mine, it was apparent that they constantly disagreed with each other. Hugh Williams complained that he was receiving slight assistance from John Pugh. Every payment was to be paid in halves, with each partner paying his exact half; even the wages were paid in halves on separate days, whilst income from the sale of lead ore to the smelters was also divided in halves in the same way.

By the 1830s the Llechwedd Ddu engine shaft had been sunk at least 50–60 yards, and the mine manager was a Mr Edward Davies, who had received his training at the Parys Mountain Copper mine and had recently taken a lease of the Rhoswydol mine and, later, the Dyfngwm mines and the Radnorshire mine of Nant y Car. Transportation costs were still high, with the cost of transporting timber alone at 20s per ton.

By 1845 Dylife was returning 70 tons of lead and 10–12 tons of copper monthly. In 1848, John Pugh died, bequeathing large debts to his wife, who resided at 2, Craig y Don, Aberdyfi. It is said that he spent much of his share of the profits from Dylife in nearby Caelan mines, investing £9,000 in three years. It was also in this year that Hugh Williams, who was involved in the Rebecca and Chartist movements, was chief speaker at the first Chartist meeting on the coalfield near Merthyr.

In 1849, Mrs Pugh's inability to put money into the mine and the men not being paid on a regular monthly basis gave rise to difficulties. In March 1849, Hugh Williams had a stroke while at the mine with Mathew Francis, who was surveying for a report. From this point on (October 1849), Hugh William's son John acted for him regarding the mines (C.J. Williams). Mathew Francis was a mining engineer, originally from Cornwall, who since 1834 had worked in Wales for John Taylor and Sons. Following his dismissal in 1842, he turned towards consultancy and promotional work.

From the report prepared by Mathew Francis it is evident that at this time the main activity at Dylife was centred on the Llechwedd Ddu lode, where the engine shaft had been sunk to the 45 fathom level, although the lode at this point was very poor. However, to the east and west the lode was found to be very productive for a length of 80 fathoms, in many places yielding three or four tons of lead with a few hundredweights of copper to the cubic fathom. Francis also noticed that the lode split into three branches towards the west.

In 1849, the old workings extended 200 fathoms through the Esgairgaled and Pencerrig properties. Francis advised further increasing the depth of the Esgairgaled shaft, which was then only

20 fathoms deep, and enlarging and extending Level Goch (Red level) on the area believed to be the confluence of the Llechwedd Ddu and Esgairgaled lodes. To compensate for the rapid growth of the mines, Francis suggested the construction of several large reservoirs and other surface developments, and the completion of a cross cut north from Llechwedd Ddu engine shaft at the 25 fathom level to connect with the Gwaith Gwyn workings on the Esgairgaled lode, a distance of about 40 fathoms. The cross cut had been started ten years earlier but abandoned because the water wheel for pumping was inadequate and it was feared that the workings would flood. The level was driven through hard ground, cutting the Esgairgaled lode at a point where it was nine fathoms wide, although no ore worth valuing was discovered and it was abandoned until 1861, when a large body of ore was discovered west of the cross cut.

The pumping machinery operating at Dylife in the year 1849 consisted of a waterwheel, 37 feet in diameter; this was probably situated on the north side of the stream, close to the engine shaft at Esgairgaled. The same wheel also pumped at Llechwedd Ddu shaft, via a long run of flat rods that passed in front of Esgairgaled cottage. This machinery was first used on 7th June 1839; a Welsh verse was prepared especially for the occasion, to be spoken alternately by 'the engine' and the daughter of Mr Pugh:

By the Engine:

Yn gadarn mi a godaf — y dwfr
A difyr y gweithiaf,
Am filoedd y gofalaf.
Byr ddydd aiaf, hir ddydd haf.

By Miss Pughe:

> *Rhod odidog rhaid ydi — dy berchi,*
> *Dau berchen a lonni;*
> *A'r Rhodos (yn lle rhydi),*
> *Llychia o'r llawr ddŵr fel lli.*

By the Engine:

> *Maria Jones mor Ian o Liw — perffaith,*
> *O rodd odiaeth ydiw;*
> *Fy ngalw enw mor wiw*
> *Gan adel im heb edliew.*

By Miss Pughe:

> *Bodlon o'm calon coelia — fedd genyf*
> *Fe ganaf o fawrdra;*
> *Sylw o'r enw bara,*
> *Fwy na'n dwy sydd ddwy oes dda.*

A waterwheel measuring 18 feet in diameter was erected on the dressing floors near the confluence of Afon Twymyn and the stream Nant Rhydwen that flows through the engine dingle, known locally as Cwm yr Engine, to provide power to the crushing mill. Drawing was achieved by the use of horse whims. Francis also advised the construction of several large waterwheels, some tram roads, and the large reservoirs previously mentioned.

Much development was taking place at Dylife in the year 1851. A 40-ft wheel was erected for crushing, whilst on the bank just below Blaen Twymyn, a wheel measuring 63 feet in diameter by 3½ feet width, was erected for pumping and drawing at Llechwedd Ddu engine shaft, replacing the long run of flat rods from

Esgairgaled. This wheel was known as Rhod Goch (Red wheel) or Martha wheel; it must have been the largest in Wales and one of the largest in Britain, similar in size even to the Lady Isabella wheel at Laxey, on the Isle of Man. It was supplied with water by a large reservoir known as Rhyd y Porthmyn Pool that was built at the western end of the village. A row of miner's cottages, known as Rhanc y Mynydd, was under construction, and, to the north a reservoir, Llyn Nant Ddeiliog, provided water to Rhod Goch and to Rhod Ddu at Esgairgaled. According to David Bick, the latter was the 1839 wheel, which was moved from Esgairgaled and repositioned by the side of the road to take advantage of the new leat system. All these modifications were carried out under the direction of the much respected and well known mining personality, Captain Edward Williams, who managed the mine for Williams and Pugh from 1830 to 1856. At this point in the grand history of Dylife, output was exceeding 1,000 tons. On April 28th, 1852, Williams & Pugh entertained their 300 men, women and children employees with tea, coffee and cold meat on the occasion of Sir Watkin William Wynn's marriage.

Displeased with Mrs Pugh's lack of financial input, in 1852, John Williams wrote a series of letters of complaint to her Trustees, David Howell, a solicitor from Machynlleth, and the Revd. Benjamin Morgan of Aberdyfi. However, the situation did not improve; later that year, as C. J. Williams writes, 'The men were not working full eight hour shifts, the ore washers had gone on strike due to lack of payment, whilst John Williams claimed that Captain Edward Williams (Mine Captain) was inefficient and that two captains were needed as well as a clerk and a time keeper.'

Hugh Williams senior died on 14th May 1852; his funeral was

attended by Richard Cobden, as well as members of the family. In 1853, John Williams retired from business in London and started to take a more active interest in Dylife. He despaired of ever being able to reach an agreement with Mrs Pugh, who still continued to reap benefits from the mine although she contributed nothing. Meanwhile, her solicitor, Howell, stalled the articles by quibbling over points of law (C. J. Williams). Weary of dispute and frustrated negotiation, in May of 1854, John Williams handed matters over to Richard Cobden; Cobden had married Hugh Williams's daughter in 1840 and had played a part in the background of mine affairs

A shaft kibble retrieved from the bottom of the Rhilog tips. Now at a nearby farm

for several years.

Cobden called on another Hugh Williams, the auditor of the Wynnstay Estate, to insist that proper accounts should be kept, and to point out that there was an outstanding bill for gunpowder from the East Cornwall Gun Powder Co. for the sum of £127 for the previous year, of which Mrs Pugh had not paid her half. On 13th January 1856 the day came for the lease to expire. Cobden, Hugh

Richard Cobden, 1804–1865

and John Williams applied to the Court of Chancery for an order for an account of the mines. C. J. Williams writes '…that under the Court Order all monies were to be paid into Machynlleth bank and only when a credit balance of £300 was reached could any surplus be divided among the partners.' At this point, John Taylor was appointed Manager. This was not to be a happy time at Dylife, I gather there was much dispute and that output had dropped also, whilst later in 1856, a ship bringing a consignment of blasting powder was so delayed by contrary winds that the miners were thrown out of work for a fortnight. Later that year prospects were beginning to look better; in June, Jane Williams (Widow to Hugh Williams) wrote a letter to Mathew Francis:

This old postcard shows the Martha wheel with Rhanc y Mynydd in the background. Note the stands of flatrods and wire rope en route to Llechwedd Ddu engine shaft.

> I went to the works on Friday last and was glad to find the prospects brightening. The lost sheep at Llechwedd Ddu has been found, a very good bunch of ore having been cut in the 75 fathom level...

However, despite this discovery, in the first year £1,360 was spent on improvements with a loss of £868. Taylor estimated that £4,000 was needed to bring the mine up to scratch.

Mrs Pugh continued to be a problem, threatening to sell her shares to John Taylor & Sons. Things could not go on as they were and, at a meeting in London on 4th February 1857, Hugh Williams, the Auditor, produced an order for the sale of the mine.

Richard Cobden, who did not like Mrs Pugh and described her as a 'Wild Woman', fought hard to stop the mine falling into

John Bright, M.P. 1811–1889

the hands of John Taylor, who, because he was Sir Watkin's Mineral Agent and possibly held shares, was well placed to take control.

Cobden called upon his friend and fellow politician, John Bright. John Bright was an M.P for Birmingham, although he had previously been an M.P of Manchester from 1843 to 1857 and was well connected there, despite losing his seat when he became unpopular for opposing the Crimean War. Bright was also a Quaker and a successful cotton manufacturer. Although Cobden was originally from Sussex, he had done very well for himself and by 1832 was living in an affluent part of Manchester. He was a radical politician, a campaigner for free trade, and had, on various occasions, campaigned for causes that would improve the lives of the working classes. Like Bright, whom he must have known for quite some time, owing to their similar political leanings, he was much opposed to the Corn Laws that made corn and, therefore, bread expensive.

Cobden's efforts were to prove very successful and, on 4th September 1858, Bright and his Manchester associates signed a lease and purchased the mine for the sum of £24,000.

The new Dylife Mining Co. Limited was formed, chaired by John Bright. It was registered on 7th July 1858, with 336 shares of £100 each, of which 318 had been sold by the end of January

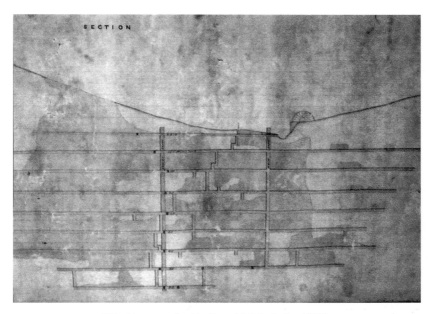

Workings on the Llechwedd Ddu lode, 1857

1859. Cobden invested in 10 shares, his wife eventually owned 6. Later in 1859, Cobden, now free of the troubles that had beset him over the last few years, set off for the USA, to investigate affairs in the Illinois Central Railway, in which he also had shares.

The new company made many great changes to the mine, some of which included fitting a double decked cage with Aytoun's patent safety catches to Llechwedd Ddu engine shaft. This was operated by a one-inch diameter steel wire with a breaking strain of 27 tons. Later, a cage was also fitted to Bradford's Shaft. In about 1861, an inspector engaged upon an extensive survey of all British mines was able to report:

> I consider the whole of the winding machinery to be the most perfect to be found in the metallic mines visited.

Dyliffe Mines

List of the Shareholders of The Dyliffe
Mining Company

Names	Amount of Shares
	£
J. B. Smith Esqre M P Westminster Terrace Hyde Park	4,000
James Vaughan Esqre Gloucester Terrace	2,000
John Bright Esqre M P Rochdale	4,000
Samson Ricardo Esqre Petworth Park nr Windsor	4,000
Joseph Locke Esqre M P Lowndes Square	2,000
William Hargreaves Esqre Craven Hill Gardens	4,000
Thomas Roberts Esqre Manchester	2,000
Edward Walker Esqre Do	1,000
William Bradford Esqre Do	1,000
Nathaniel Buckley Esqre Ashton under Lyne	1,000
Dr Frankland Bartholomew Hospital	500
Newton Heath &c	2,500
	£28000

and £5,600 more to be raised pro rata and
expended during the first seven years on the
development of the Mine making with £14000
paid of the £28000 the sum of £9,600 to be
expended

* This Firm was mentioned by Mr Taylor as
willing to take one fourth or one sixth of the
mine. If they decline other parties are ready to
take the amount

List of shareholders, New Company, 1858

Dyliffe Mines Cost

From March 15th to April 3rd 1858. (3 weeks)

Agents' Salaries

Edward Williams	salary	½ month	5. 0. 0			
James Hughes	do	½ "	2. 10. 0		7 10 .

Llechweddu

Tutwork Accounts

Edward Roberts & 5 ptrs. driving the 55 fms. level west of the Engine Shaft. 7 ft. high by 5 ft. wide with dead levels in the Lode fms. 2. 0. 10 @ £4 . . 8. 11. 1

Deduct Materials	3. 17. 9		
Doctor	. 3 .	4. 0. 9	4. 10. 4

Richard Morris & 5 ptrs. driving the 75 fm. level west of the Engine Shaft. 7 ft. high by 5 ft. wide with dead levels in the Lode; fms. 5. 3. 6 @ £3 . . . 16. 15. 0

Deduct Materials	5. 10. 5		
Doctor	3. 0	5. 13. 5	11. 1. 7

John Jervis & 5 ptrs. driving the 75 fm. level east of the Whim Shaft 7 ft. high by 5 ft. wide with dead levels in the Lode fms. 1. 5. 5 @ £5. 17. 6 | 11. 3. 7

Deduct Materials	3. 13. 2		
Doctor	3. 0	3. 16. 2	7. 7. 5

Carried on	22. 19. 4	7 10 .

1858 sheet of accounts

The Llechwedd Ddu Shaft Cage, Llywernog Mining Museum

It is worth mentioning at this point that Dylife was the only mine in Wales to provide changing rooms. At other mines, men walked to and from work in their underground working clothes. This development probably went a long way to reduce illness amongst the miners at Dylife.

The new company also decided to make a determined attack on the Dylife lode; this resulted in an engine shaft being sunk on

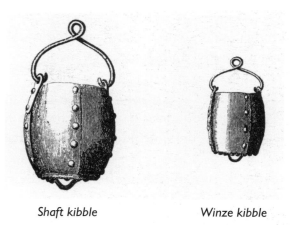

Shaft kibble   Winze kibble

the Dylife/Dyfngwm boundary (Boundary Shaft). Once this shaft was sunk to the 35 fathom level, a crosscut was driven through the lode and a nice run of lead ore was discovered, which continued to run down through all the levels to the bottom of the present workings.

Another important development at this time was the sinking of Bradford Shaft, so-named after the company's managing director, in order to exploit workings on the Llechwedd Ddu lode, where the engine shaft was down to the 85fathom level. Bradford Shaft was well situated, conveniently close to the dressing floors, allowing ore from the lowermost workings to be trammed directly to the dressing floors. Standard wagons were introduced, which measured 3ft, 6in x 2ft, 6in x 20in deep. I understand that these were made in Manchester at a cost of £5 each.

It is worthy of note that these shaft cages were of the utmost importance in Dylife's history, creating a much more efficient method of raising ore, and setting Dylife far apart from other mines in the vicinity that were still raising ore by kibble. In 1970,

David Bick excavated a part of the Llechwedd Ddu shaft cage, which had somehow become removed and buried downstream. This relic is now preserved alongside other mining artefacts in the Llywernog Mining Museum.

In 1860 prospects at Dylife were looking good, with the mine producing as much as 200 tons a month and being mentioned in a government report as the only mine of any importance east of Plynlimon.

In August 1860 a waterwheel measuring 50 feet x 6 feet was constructed, for drawing at Old Engine Shaft and, later, Boundary Shaft; the wheel pit had to be carved out of solid rock and erection was not completed until 1861. The site is about 450 yards south, south-east of the Star Inn and only a stone's throw below the mountain road. Although the wheel pit is largely filled in, the position of the drawing machine can be seen alongside, it was once housed in a small building with a chimney on the east side. Most mid Wales drawing machine houses had a fireplace, if for no other reason than the comfort of the attendant who would have to operate the equipment through all of the seasons. (The Martha wheel drawing house was also equipped with a fireplace.) Access was achieved via a short track from the road above and then a small footbridge across the leat. From the drawing machine, a wire rope, supported on posts and rollers, ran right over Dylife mountain.

In 1992 I uncovered one of these posts, with a roller still intact; upon further inspection in 1999, I was saddened to find it had been removed, probably to a private collection somewhere. The cable, when it reached the top of Dylife hill, passed beneath the old coach road about 200 yards east of Pen y Crogbren; the spot is still marked by a gulley and culvert. According to David Bick,

Carved out of the rock – the 50 x 6 ft wheelpit.
The position of the drawing machine is clearly visible alongside

the whole must have formed the longest and most powerful water-operated drawing equipment in Great Britain. I understand that the local postman earned a shilling or two by oiling the rollers. An extra length of rope was added at Old Engine Shaft, to enable drawing at Boundary Shaft, although this was probably not until the 1870s, as an old mine plan of 1869 shows a horse whim drawing from there.

1862 was to prove Dylife's best year, with 2,571 tons of lead ore sold, making profits of £1000 a month, I gather that the majority of ore sold was taken from the Llechwedd Ddu lode. With the later exception of the Van Mine near Llanidloes, this was to prove the greatest annual output of any mine in mid Wales.

With regard to working conditions in 1863, I gather from evidence then collected for a Government report that there were 250 men working underground at Dylife, of which the Dylife lode accounted for 38. Fourteen men were working the Esgairgaled lode at its eastern and western ends down to the 40 fathom level. Ventilation was achieved by blowing machines operated by boys turning a handle. This report also mentioned that the cottages were overcrowded (David Bick).

In 1864 Dylife's population totalled about a thousand people, served by three inns, a church and three chapels. Until 1864 all the lead ore was taken to Derwenlas, a small port situated several miles south of Machynlleth, on the edge of the Dyfi estuary. It was capable of accommodating vessels up to 70 tons at two ports there, namely Cei Ward and Cei Ellis, and at one time as many as 80 vessels at a time were reported to ride the tides of the Dyfi up to Derwenlas. Many of the farmers in Dylife were paid a retaining fee of £1 a month to be ready on call to cart the ore to Derwenlas, a distance of 12 miles, to ensure that the big ships would have a full load. From April 15th, 1860, until the beginning of 1862, 805 tons of lead ore from Dylife were shipped from Derwenlas.

1864 saw great changes in the way all future consignments of ore would leave Dylife as it was in this year that the railway from Aberystwyth to Shrewsbury was opened, passing through Llanbrynmair. All transport of lead ore from Dylife to Derwenlas ceased and on 20th December 1863, the last cargo of ore – amounting to 35 tons – was consigned by the Dylife and Dyfngwm mines and dispatched in the hold of a sloop called the *Seven Brothers* that sailed from Cei Ward. Not only was this to be the last ore from Dylife to be sent by sea, but this was the last vessel and cargo to leave Cei Ward before its closure, owing to the popularity of the railway.

An interesting cutting from a newspaper article in the 1860s read:

Derwenlas Port

Interesting figures of the trade at the once prosperous port of Derwenlas were given by a Mr John Jones of Glanmerin at a meeting of the County Council Finance Committee, at which it was decided to apply to the road board for a grant for the construction of a bridge across the Dyfi near Llugwy to avoid a detour of 7 miles. In 1847 Mr Jones said the trade of the port was: Exports, 500 tons of bark, 40,000ft of timber, 150,000 ft of oak poles for collieries, 1,500 tons of slate. Imports: 5000qrs of rye and wheat, 1000 tons of coal, 2000 tons of limestone, 11000 English and foreign hides and goods to the value £14000. Mr Jones also quoted figures that 586 tons of lead ore were produced from the lead mines of Dylife in 1845.

As well as being a key port on the Dyfi for import and export, Derwenlas, for a while, played an important part in the shipping industry on the river with as many as 14 vessels being built there between 1840 and 1880, exceeded only by the shipbuilders of Aberdyfi, who are recorded to have produced 46 vessels in the same period.

It is said that, before the mountain road to Machynlleth was modernized with a tarmac surface, in several places cart tracks could be seen worn into the rock; a testimony to all the carts of lead that had passed that way, on route to Derwenlas.

When Sir Watkin Williams Wynne took the mine into his hands, he constructed a new road from Dylife, to the Staylittle

– Llanbrynmair road (this is the mountain road that we use today that goes past the waterfall down to the T junction), so that all the ore could be transported to Llanbrynmair Station, a distance of 8 miles from Dylife. He also had a shed built close to the station for storing the ore. In 1880 it was suggested that a narrow gauge line be built to connect Dylife with Machynlleth but the times were against such a scheme and nothing was done.

When Richard Cobden died in April 1865, workings at Llechwedd Ddu were down to the 115 fathom level and prospects were looking bad. The lead in the engine shaft had become increasingly scarce from the 60 fathom level downwards. The best run of ore had been to the east of the shaft, about 20 fathoms along. Some of these levels above the lode were found to contain 18 inches of solid lead, although this was not the case in the bottom levels, where the ground was said to contain more shale, and by 1867 output had slowly began to fall. Realising that the mine had been exhausted, Bright and friends decided to dispose of the mine in its entirety for the sum of £73,000, which was not a bad figure, considering they only paid £24,000 for the mine 15 years earlier and had, most probably, taken the best of the ore out. At this time, a correspondent for the *Mining Journal* said that "Not an end in the mine would produce one cwt per fathom".

The new company chairman was a Mr Offley Bohun Shore and the manager a Mr Ralph Dean, the latter remaining manager until his death in 1881. The new company took over in 1873 and put much money towards new developments above and below ground. Work was centred on the Dylife lode, Boundary Shaft was sunk to the 132 fathom level and a skip road was installed. At Pencerrig, the deep adit was pushed east a considerable distance,

The dressing floor area, 1870s. 1) Double launders 2) Chimney to horizontal puffer 3) Mine office 4) Headframe, Bradfords Shaft 5) Blackwheel

and a short crosscut driven from the Llechwedd Ddu Shaft at the 105 fathom level in an attempt to meet with the Esgairgaled lode, although none of these developments seemed to meet with much success.

In 1869, Dylife was mentioned in the first of three booklets published by Liscombe and Co., a company from Liverpool. According to Simon Hughes of SJS Mining Services, Talybont, the purpose of the booklet was probably as a handout to potential investors in the mines, with a view to enticing them to undertake a transaction through Liscombe's business. As can be seen from the report, little or no attention is given to machinery, output or current state of the mine:

DYLIFFE

Lies about eight miles north-west of Llanidloes in a
direct line, but ten miles by the road from that town
to Machynlleth; this property has been worked for
many years and is celebrated for the large returns it has
made. It is generally understood that John Bright, Esq.
MP here realised a great portion of his fortune. The
mine of late has not been quite so rich as in past years,
but there is no doubt that further development will
discover resources equally as valuable as the deposits
worked through.

With regard to machinery in 1874, when the agents were E
Evans and E Rogers, the 50 x 6-foot wheel was still drawing at
Boundary Shaft and Old Engine Shaft at Pen Dylife. A 20-inch
engine with two six-ton boilers aided the Red Wheel, whilst at
Boundary Shaft there was a 60-inch Cornish Pumping Engine of
9-foot stroke, of equal beam, together with two ten-ton boilers.
In the four weeks ending 7th September 1878 the engine house
was cleaned and whitewashed and 4½ days were spent packing the
piston. This work was normally done by two brothers, William
and Henry Goldsworthy (David Bick). The engine was housed
in a three-storey building with a tall chimney. Such a powerful
engine attached to such a long run of pump rods would have caused
quite a strain on the pit work and, at some point, a balance bob
was fitted at the 150 fathom level, the total depth for this shaft
eventually becoming 167 fathoms, making it the deepest shaft in
mid Wales. The engine ceased work in January 1880, when the
cost of transporting coal to fuel it proved to be uneconomical.
This engine appears to have stood derelict for many years and was
still standing unused in 1903, before eventually being taken away
for scrap some years later.

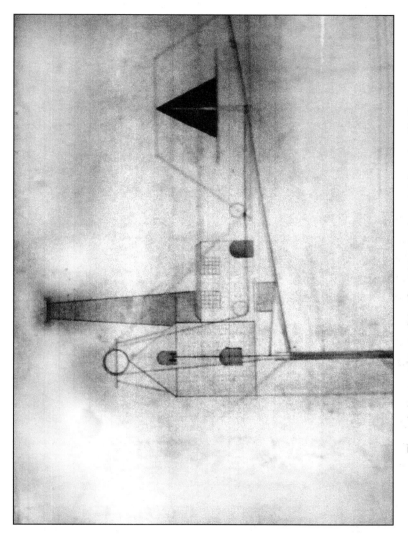

The only known picture of the Cornish engine house at Boundary Shaft.
Note also the horse whim and balance box

THE

GREAT DYLIFFE MINING COMPANY,

LIMITED.

Incorporated under the Companies' Acts, 1862, 1867 and 1877,
Whereby the liability of the Shareholders is limited to the amount of their Shares.

Capital, £20,000, in 20,000 Shares of £1 each,

FULLY PAID UP.

FIRST ISSUE, 13,000 SHARES.

London Offices, 20, *Moorgate Street, E.C.*

THIS Company has been formed for the purpose, among other things, of purchasing the Lease or Leases of the Mines, known as the Dyliffe, Llechwedd-du and Esgairgaled Mines, situate in the Parishes of Penegoes and Darowen, in the County of Montgomery, together with the Engines, Machinery, Plant and Materials appertaining thereto.

This run of Mines is one of the most extensive in Wales, and up to the period of the great discoveries made at the Van Mine, was considered the most productive in Montgomeryshire, the sett being nearly two miles in length by about the same in width, and in it, three lodes or veins (besides branches) have been proved and worked upon, viz:—the Dyliffe, Llechwedd-du and Esgairgaled lodes. The former is about 600 yards to the South of either of the others, there being no underground communication between it and them, practically, therefore, they form two separate Mines, the Dyliffe Mine, and the Llechwedd-du and Esgairgaled Mine, the latter being worked by shafts sunk on the Llechwedd-du lode, and by cross-cuts from these to the Esgairgaled lode.

In addition to these, is what has been termed the "new lode," a discovery branching from the adit level of Dyliffe, which, so far as seen, is a strong and well mineralized lode; the working on this was suspended for want of funds in May, 1878.

A very important feature in the working of these Mines, is the great saving of expense, through the use of water-power, the Mines being provided with very effective water-wheels, one of which is believed to be one of the largest in the Kingdom, two of the others being of large size, 45 and 50 ft. in diameter. A good supply of water exists from large lakes or reservoirs collecting and storing the water, so that few Mines can be worked so economically, in this respect, as the Dyliffe.

Labour is very cheap and abundant, and there is ample machinery at all points of the most improved description, including a very powerful pumping engine, sawmill, and the general plant for pumping, winding, crushing and dressing ore. The Mines are making good monthly returns of ore, and are taken over as a going concern.

Prospectus 1878 (Denbighshire Record Office)

38

On the dressing floors were two large waterwheels, one of which was the 1851, 40-ft crushing wheel, driving two crushers, a stonebreaker and revolving colrakes and jiggers. The other drove six revolving buddles and a zenor buddle. In addition to this there was a 12-inch horizontal engine with a 5-ton boiler, as a standby.

In the next few years things did not improve and, in 1876, the company reformed but there was little hope for recovery. In 1878 ore at Dylife was priced at about £9 a ton. In 1879 another new company took over and, in a desperate attempt to find a good deposit of ore, work on all three lodes began; hope was rekindled when a foot of galena was revealed by sinking a shaft on one of the new lodes (Alfred's Shaft – named after the managing director, a Mr H. J. Alfred). This new lode had been discovered when driving the great Dylife adit but had not been explored. Unfortunately, the deposit proved of little substance and work on this shaft was abandoned. Later, an attempt was made to sink the Llechwedd Ddu Shaft below the 105 fathom level, but this petered out due to lack of funds. From 1878–1881, the numbers of men employed at Dylife had gradually fallen from 109 to 70, and the average monthly wage for the miner was barely £3. In 1884 the company collapsed, and the mine was closed, after working non stop since the late 18th century. I gather from the late Will Richards that the company left Wales and went to try their luck in Nevada, and that they were the last registered company to work the Dylife mine. In the two years to follow, mining was carried on in a half-hearted fashion by local miners, who continued to raise small quantities of ore; 192 tons to be returned in 1885. These consignments were sent to Swansea via Llanbrynmair.

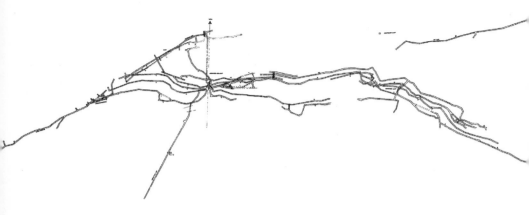

Plan of workings, Llechwedd Ddu and Esgairgaled lodes, 1877

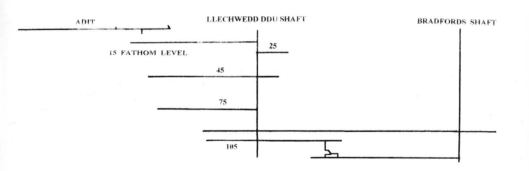

ADIT
LLECHWEDD DDU SHAFT
BRADFORDS SHAFT
15 FATHOM LEVEL
25
45
75
105

A section of workings on the Llechwedd Ddu lode, 1877

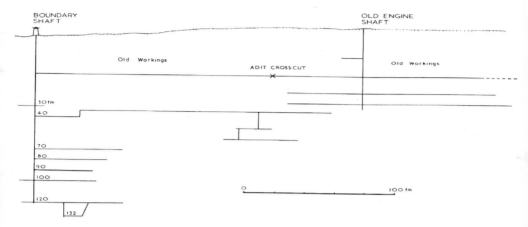

A section of workings on the Dylife lode, 1877. Re-drawn by David Bick, from an original by Isaac Shone Wrexham

Plan of workings on Dylife lode, 1877. Boundary shaft is to the left, the old engine shaft to the right, and the adit crosscut is in the middle.

Before I continue, I will spend a little time on the history of the Rhod Goch. This wheel was erected in 1851 and it is said that it worked for 50 years without a break. During the time it worked at Dylife, its job was to draw from Esgairgaled and pump and draw from Llechwedd Ddu Engine Shaft. It later drew from Bradford's Shaft. To ease the load on the waterwheel, the drawing machine consisted of one drum for each shaft, so arranged that one cage descended as the other rose. The two drums had different diameters, to cater for the different shaft depths. Water was applied to the wheel via a sluice in the launder, operated by a cable in the drawing house. Towards the end of the 19th century, the outer ends of the wooden spokes of Rhod Goch had rotted quite seriously and, to avoid the cost of replacing them, the decaying ends of the spokes were cut off, thus reducing the diameter of the wheel to 60 feet. This would account for the step in the launder, as seen in the picture on the front cover. Following the closure of the mines, I do not know when the wheel was removed, or what became of it. More than likely, it was scrapped, but it must have stood idle for quite some time, perhaps being demolished in 1911, along with most of the other surface features. An interesting story to relate is that, during the time of the 2nd World War, along the side of the mountain road were bundles of barbed wire, the idea being that they could be strung out in the event of an invasion, to halt any German advance. However, when the war was over and they had not been needed, the wire was discarded and thrown into the then empty wheel pit of the Red Wheel. Beneath the farm rubbish that was put there later, it is probably still there today.

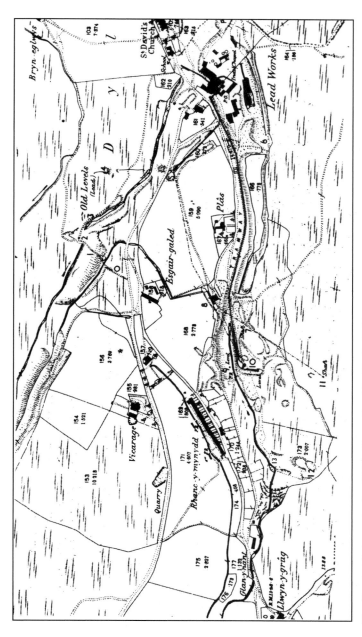

The Esgairgaled area in the 1880s (As outlined by Mr D. Bick)

0) Site of Black Wheel; 1) Footway shaft; 2) Esgairgaled shaft & tunnel for stream; 3) Pencerrig deep adit; 4) Pencerrig shallow adit; 5) Bradford's Shaft; 6) Shaft on south lode; 7) Footway shaft; 8) 63ft Red Wheel; 9) Gwaith Gwyn adit; 10) Llechwedd Ddu engine shaft and Dylife adit; 11) Alfred's shaft; 12) Junction of lodes; 13) Level Goch

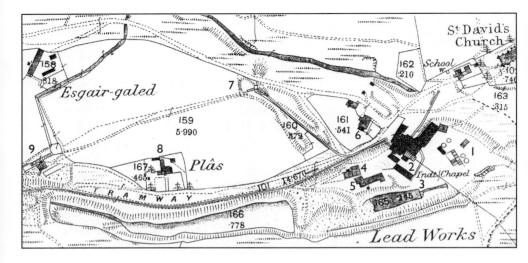

Dressing floor area, 1887. 1) Water wheel and buddles; 2) crushing wheel;
3) Capel Coed; 4) Post Office with blacksmith's next door; 5) company stables;
6) mine office; 7) Bradford's shaft; 8) manager's house; 9) Red Wheel

From 1886–1891, a local man, Evan Evans, who had worked in the mine for many years, restarted work at Dylife under the name of Blaen Twymyn, and he resided in the house of that name. Twenty to thirty men found employment and several hundred tons of lead and zinc were raised. There was much blende in the Esgairgaled lode but the hard nature of the veinstone and the low value of blende went a long way to restricting output. No copper ore was returned in these years, although a considerable amount of copper pyrites was found in the Llechwedd Ddu lode and, in 1892, 14 tons of ore were raised from an old working east of Dylife (most likely the workings I uncovered at Nant y Maes). One of the farmers carting lead around this time was Owen Hughes of Dyfngwm Isaf, who, when required, would take two horses with carts of lead to Llanbrynmair Station. On his return journey, he brought back food for other farms' animals, and left it at nearby Hirnant Farm before he returned home.

About 1900, Evans laid a tram road from Esgairgaled Engine Shaft to the dressing floors, crossing the road via a wooden bridge. This railway would have undoubtedly followed the course of an earlier tram road to the floors. Evans had kept Dylife going for 10–15 years, but in 1900 he was short of capital and the lodes were running very poor. In addition to this, the expense of keeping the mine dry proved to be too much and he had to give it up. All working at Dylife ceased in 1901, and, after over a century of activity, the mine became flooded.

In 1908, a Mr John Saurey of Bucklersbury was in negotiation for a take-note of the mineral rights to the estate, although the matter was not pursued as Mr Saurey died suddenly. Prior to Mr Saurey's death, he had formed a company to re-open Dylife. His intended plan of action was the grand task of driving a tunnel, a mile in length, from the base of the Pennant rock, to drain Dylife to within 10 fathoms of the deepest workings; he had a 42-year lease, dated 1907, from Sir Watkin W. Wynn.

There is some reference to miners picking over the waste tips in 1913 but the last real activity at Dylife took place in the late 1920s, when a company, going by the name of Hirnant Minerals, owned by a Mr John Stevens of Brierley Hill, Birmingham, attempted to rework the enormous dumps below the mountain road in 1926. These waste tips were known as Rhilog and were optimistically estimated to contain 10,000 tons of lead ore. Hirnant Minerals set up a small dressing plant by the roadside (the foundations of which can still be seen today) about 200 yards south-east of the Star

DYLIFE MINE.

DEAR SIR,

This Mine is situated about 9 miles to the S. East of Machynlleth, in the County of Montgomery, and about 6 miles to the South of Llanbrynmair.

The formation is the Upper Silurian. The grant embraces over 600 acres, and it is a mile long on the course of the E. & West Lodes.

It is traversed by 5, E. & West Lodes, which naming them in the order of occurrence from North to South are as follows :—

1. Esgirgaled.
2. Llechwedd-du.
3. Intermediate Lode, dipping North (New).
4. Do. do. do. South (New).
5. Dylife, or Dyfngwm Lode.

Only 3 Lodes have hitherto been worked, viz., 1, 2 and 5, and each proved remarkably rich the profits in the aggregate, having been more than a quarter of a million pounds sterling. In one year the balance to the credit of the company which formerly worked it, with which the late Messrs Cobden & Bright, were closely associated exceeded £20000. The monthly returns of Lead Ore averaging 300 tons. In the Llechwedd-du Lode, No. 2, there are nice runs of Ore going down below the bottom level, 300 yards deep, and the deeper development of this, as well as of the Dylife and Esgirgaled Lodes, offers a fair chance of success. But the greatest importance is attached to the results that are expected to attend the development of the Virgin Lodes, 3 and 4, situated between the Llechwedd-du and Dylife Lodes, which can be undertaken and carried out at a comparative small cost, by driving a crosscut at a depth of 70 fms. exploring them therefrom. These Lodes 3 and 4, are well defined on surface and each shows a little Ore, looking quite as well as the other Lodes which proved so rich, and in my opinion there can scarcely be a doubt that if developed in depth they will prove very rich. A corresponding trial at the "Van Mine," situated in the same Geological formation, about 6 miles to the S. East, has resulted in a great success. A crosscut has been driven South, and a New Lode has been discovered which is very rich.

The Mine is thoroughly equipped with Pumping, Winding, and Dressing Machinery of a Modern description, all worked by Waterpower, the cost of which would be several thousands of pounds. It has capacious Workshops supplied with good tools, and there are plenty of Rails and Materials which will suffice for all requirements for a considerable period. The Annual Rent for the Waterpower is only £6, and the Royalty but $\frac{1}{24}$th. with a redeemable dead rent of only £10 a year.

The standing charges for keeping the Mine drained and in working order are very small, and inasmuch as the length of the crosscut would not exceed 200 yards, to intersect the two Lodes which can be driven at £3 a yard. The cost of the important trial indicated would not exceed £1400, after allowing a fair sum for the exploration of the Lodes after they have been intersected.

I propose the formation of a syndicate holding shares in multiples of £100 each, to raise £2000, and to show my confidence in the property, I am prepared to take one share.

I have great confidence that before twelve months elapse, a substantial discovery would be made, and it is probable that ere then there will be improvement in the price of Lead, either of which happening would admit of a formation of "Limited Liability Co.," to take the property over at a substantial profit to the syndicate.

I have visited the property on three occasions and have incurred considerable expense in making myself acquainted with the facts of the case, but I do not ask to be recouped, and I shall be quite content to join the syndicate, on the same terms as are conceded to others.

I am, Dear Sir,

Yours truly,

MATTHEW FRANCIS.

(*Signed*)

A prospectus dating from an attempt to sell Dylife in 1894

Inn. A Blackstone 45-horsepower diesel engine was installed to operate the concentrating plant. The lead and zinc was taken by lorry to Llanbrynmair and from there by train to Newcastle-on-Tyne. Will Richards was employed as a lorry driver and ore dresser. However, by 1930, it was decided that the dumps were not yielding the expected returns and the operation ceased. The manager was an elderly Scotsman by the name of Mr Wallace, who had spent much of his time as a mining engineer in New Zealand. Tommy Wilson relates, "He was a very nice gentleman who kept very much to himself, a no nonsense chap, his work being top priority." He and his wife

A vice in a shed at a house in Dolgadfan that is said to have come from Dylife

rented two rooms at the Vicarage. At this time, Hirnant Minerals were making an attempt to re-open the main adit of Dyfngwm mine in a neighbouring valley and it was to here that the Blackstone engine along with other plant was removed. I am informed by Mrs Gwen Rees that the powder house, *Carfen y Pwdr*, at this time stood to the left of the mountain road just by where the cart track from Pen Dylife joins it and not all that far from where the post-box is today. There was also a sign bearing the name Hirnant Minerals painted on a zinc sheet that was left behind. I understand it eventually became removed to nearby Rhiwdyfeitty

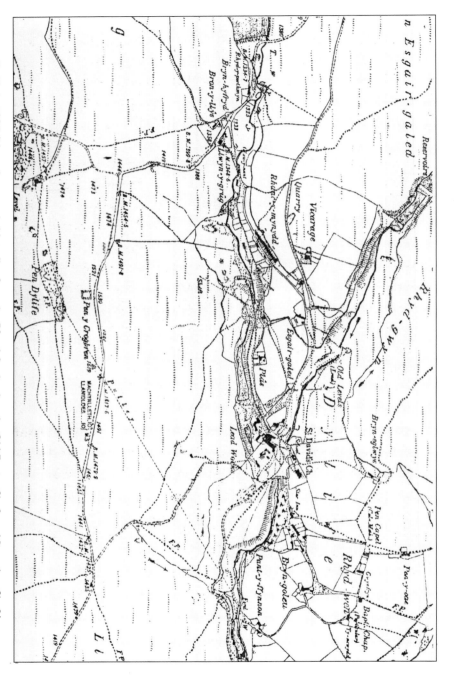

Dylife in 1885 (Note the remarkable pulley from the 50 x 6 ft wheel to the Old Engine Shaft and Boundary Shaft)

farm, although my best efforts to locate it have failed.

It is worth mentioning that, prior to moving to Dyfngwm, Hirnant Minerals cleared out the Great Dylife Adit with the intention of providing direct underground access to Dyfngwm; however, Alfred's Shaft collapsed, completely blocking the adit.

The old shed that survives opposite the Star Inn is nothing to do with the mine, as often assumed, but is the remains of a weighbridge that was erected in 1963. At this time, stone was being taken from the tips (that used to extend across the valley floor as far as the river) for use in the initial construction stages of the Clywedog Dam. The hauler was a Mr D M Williams of Machynlleth, who ran a fleet of 12 Dodge trucks to take the stone to the dam site. The trucks, which ran alternately, were loaded by hand, the stone was bought onto a concrete platform by a drot, and from there one man shovelled it into a lorry below, and, unlikely as it sounds, I am assured this was the method. It must have been a back-breaking task.

The dumps between the Star Inn and the Machynlleth road are of special, mineralogical interest and, in geological terms, fine specimens of banded sulphide ore (sphalerite-galena) can still be found, hemimorphite being a cimmin alteration product of the sphalerite. The main interest, however, lies in the fact that the zone of supergene alteration was at least partly intact at the time of mining and that this is one of the few places in Wales (q.v. Eaglebrook and Vaughan Mines) where a wide range of lead, zinc and copper secondary minerals is found.

2. Dylife Village

It is difficult to know when the first house was built at Dylife; certainly some of the stone farmsteads date back to at least the 1600s. From notes that came attached to the map of 1776 which appears in chapter one, it is certain that there was a dwelling at Rhyd y Porthmyn, the tenant being a Hugh Tudor of Esgairfochnant. There were also dwellings at Bryn Moel (Mr Wynn's tenement) and Rhyd Wen (Mr Lloyd's tenement). Esgairgaled (now a farm building at Blaen Twymyn) was let to a Ross Pugh.

By the 1820s houses were built in good numbers as there were so many employed at the mines. In 1845 there were 200 men employed at Llechwedd Ddu and Esgairgaled. By 1850 there was much building taking place in the village, and it was starting to grow as never before. In 1841 the Methodist chapel was built, followed by the Baptist chapel in 1852, and St David's Church in 1856. In 1857 the National School was built at a cost of £250, also a School House. The Vicarage was built in 1857, when the population in Dylife totalled 1,012. At this point, it is said, there were 92 houses or cottages in the village.

The mine around this period was certainly flourishing and it was said at one time that there were so many people working that the beds did not have time to cool between shifts. A row of houses was built on the north side of Llechwedd Ddu, which were called Rhanc y Mynydd. They consisted of 22 houses of a good size, which, by 1871, were said to be housing 123 men,

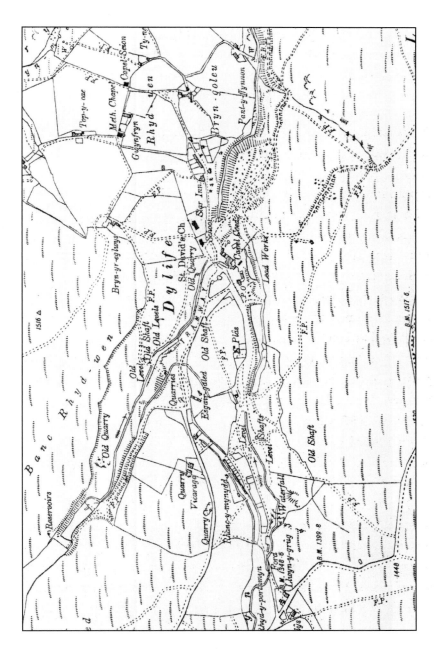

Dylife village, 1903

51

women and children. Another row was built, east of the church, which was called Bryn Goleu and consisted of 9 dwellings. Part of the wall to the rear of the Star Inn car park marks the spot where they once stood. Also, another row of four houses stood at Penfforddgerrig.

There were three public houses in the village: namely, The Star Inn, Camder Ffordd and the Drop Inn. Camder Ffordd was the oldest and it is very likely that this was in being when they were constructing the main road over Pen Dylife from Machynlleth to Llanidloes in 1770. Many years later, the licence was transferred to Llwyn y Grug Inn, which was also by the side of this road. The innkeeper not only sold beer but kept a grocery store and a butcher's shop as well as a small holding. In the 1860s, the inn was let to a Mr Williams, to run as he pleased. The Drop Inn was at the top end of the village and was frequented by the cattle drovers, who came by this way, before stopping at Rydyporthmyn to shoe the cattle and then drive them on to the lowlands. The inn is marked on the 1885 map but had been demolished by the early 1900s. The Star Inn was at the lower end of the village, about 200 yards east of St David's church, and is still run as a public house today.

The row of houses at Bryn Goleu with the Star Inn on the left

The Star Inn

Standing at 1300 feet above sea level, this is the highest pub in Wales. It is difficult to know when the Star Inn was built; part of the building dates back to 1640, although it was probably not used as an inn until much later. In the early 1900s, a William Richards was living at the Star Inn, where he remained until his death in 1918. In the 1960s, the pub was run by a Mrs Owen, an ex matron of a Cardiff hospital, who, by all accounts, was quite a character. An interesting story was told to me about a group of motorcyclists who had ridden up to the pub from Machynlleth. Mrs Owen, on seeing their red faces, wind burnt from the long ride up and thinking they had already had enough to drink, turned them away. By 1978, the pub was being run by an ex-mayor of Machynlleth, a Mr Hughes. Mr Hughes was responsible for

The Star Inn, 1950. Photograph by David Bick

53

extending the building to the size it is today and ran the pub for about 5 years.

Today, the Star Inn is run by Sue and Tony Ward Banks and their son Daniel. It has been in their hands for the last 22 years. There are two bars, one with a slate floor and open fire, which doubles as a separate dining area. Upstairs, the accommodation extends to six rooms, of varying sizes, ranging from singles to double en suite rooms.

From 1984 to 1994, the pub kept 6 horses and offered pony trekking as an alternative way of viewing the spectacular surrounding scenery. Although this is a service not available today, the stables are kept maintained, as passing trekkers occasionally stop by.

The Star Inn. Inside the bar area, 1964

Mrs Owen, landlady of the Star Inn, 1960s.
Below, the Star Inn in 2004, still going as a public house

Other visitors to the Star Inn over the years are said to have included such eminent men as Lord Snowdon and the Duke of Edinburgh. Being a regular visitor to the Star myself, I can say the food is good and the locals are a very approachable bunch, in whose company I have spent many happy times until late into the night.

★ ★ ★

The average wage for the miners in the 1800s was very low, with the men being paid 12 to 15 shillings a week for twelve hour daily shifts, whilst the women on the dressing floors were paid an average of 8 pence a day, with some of the more skilled receiving 1/- per day. The wages were paid at the end of every month, which was also a Fair day. Merchants from Machynlleth and Llanidloes brought their wares to sell, also the shoe makers of Bont, Llanbrynmair, were doing a good trade (Llanbrynmair was renowned throughout Montgomeryshire for its shoe traders), and there was a stall selling miners' hats. There was also a cock-fighting pit at Dylife, where the miners used to stake their money on their favourite fighting cocks. The location of the cockpit was in the field to the left of the track descending to Rydd y Porthmyn from the present Llanidloes to Machynlleth road. In Don Gardner's day, the ring of raised earth around which the spectators used to stand was still plainly visible, having a diameter of at least 20 yards. My best efforts to locate the site have met with disappointment and I believe it has been obscured by many years of agriculture.

The life of the miners was very short in those days. The most likely cause of premature death was the working conditions. Working long hours in places with poor ventilation, with dust and smoke from blasting combined with the sheer hard nature of the job could not have gone far to promote good health. Lewis Morris believed the fault lay within the minute particles of ore in the atmosphere, and the following extract from W J Lewis's *Lead Mining in Wales* highlights some of the problems he believed could be caused by this dust, although the report seems to concern itself more with the effects of the lead on animals than humans:

> The Creatures subject to be destroyed or are affected by it, are men, dogs, cats, horses and all Fowls: that is, Every creature that hath Lard. But those that bear Tallow Escape it. Mares are more subject to be poisoned than Geldings.
>
> Miners in some soft, dry works where the ore is free and flies in powder, are subject to a distemper in their breasts, which they feel like a heavy ball and therefore call it in Welsh *Y Belen,* i.e., The Ball. The only cure they use for it is to drink ale plentifully which they take care to do whether they have the Belen or no. Dogs that frequent about ye mines and lick up the dust with their meat are taken by fits and run about as if they were mad, but hurt nobody. At last they fall down as dead but again recover, & sometimes by giving them Butter and fat broths, get over the distemper. Cats will run mad about ye House, fasten themselves to ye top of ye House or any high place and from thence fall down as dead but generally recover.
>
> To geese ducks and hens, it is fatal, and it is in vain to attempt to keep any near a Lead mine.
>
> I have opened a Horse of mine, which died of this distemper, and found the Thorax almost full of yellow water without smell & the lungs wasted. The horses in this distemper grow lean & short breathd, & the more they are worked it is said, the better they are.

It can be seen from the headstones in the graveyard that most men died between the ages of 36 and 40.

The big sheds of the dressing floors were also used to hold

Eisteddfodau and preaching meetings. Eminent men such as Ceiriog Hughes and Mynyddog used to act as adjudicators, and the famous preacher, Herbert Evans of Caernarfon, used to preach in the big sheds.

Towards the beginning of the 1900s there were 14 small holdings around the village, all of which can be seen listed below:

Property	Acres	Rent in 1916 (per annum)
Rydd y Porthmyn	19	7-0-0
Bronllys	1	?
Llwyn y Grug Inn	11	?
Bryn Eglwys	10	8-0-0
Top y Cae	?	14-0-0
Gwynfryn	5	6-0-0
Tŷ Newydd	9	09-0-0
Pant y Ffynnon	Two holdings	09-0-0
Rydwen	Two holdings	23-0-0
Star Inn	6	07-10-0
Blaen Twymyn	Holding	
The Vicarage	Holding	

In 1915 there were several people living at Rhanc y Mynydd, namely Richard and Jane Jones (of Dylife Post Office), Hannah Richards, Evan Gwilym Davies and Wife, Margaret Hughes, Mrs Mary Corfield. The average rent of Dylife cottages in 1916 was £2-7-0 per annum.

In 1905, coal was priced at 22/- per ton, although the main fuel used was peat that was undoubtedly obtained from the Bugeilyn moors, where there was an abundance of it. (Among other vegetation, the peat largely consisted of decomposing birch; this species of tree can still be seen in the peat layers today and,

St David's Church and the school on the right, with the ruins of the Flourin on the left

many years ago, was widespread throughout the area). In 1911, Sir Watkin W. Wynne gave orders to his men to dismantle the mine in its entirety. This was systematically carried out until all the machinery and sheds were gone. Also, many of the houses were taken down, including the Plas, the manager's house. During this time Sir Watkin was building a large shooting lodge at Bugeilyn, several miles south-west of Dylife. Here he owned the large grouse moor and lakes that were with it, and I understand that many materials from the buildings at Dylife were used to construct this lodge. As Will Richards so aptly put it, "This was a crushing blow for the village and all hopes for restarting the mine vanished."

Among the dressing floors stood the congregational chapel; this was to have been taken down but the women and children of the village beat Sir Watkin's men to it, and one night they pulled it down and burnt all the timber. Sir Watkin was furious but could not find the culprits so the matter was dropped. This was the first house of worship to go. About 1950, the Baptist chapel was closed as only a few members were left, and by 1959 the population of Dylife had dwindled from 1012 to 12.

On July 9th, 1962, men started to take down St David's church, by order of the Church Authority, because it was deteriorating dangerously, and by October it had been razed to the ground. My father remembers seeing a bible on the lectern and hymnbooks on the pews, shortly before demolition. St David's church was the third place of worship to go and, in December 1966 the Methodist chapel was closed and had been sold by the following year. By 1968, there were only four inhabited houses in the village and they were: The Vicarage, Blaen Twymyn, Star Inn, and Rydwen. Will Richards relates that, at this time, six of the cottages had been bought for use as holiday homes by people from Birmingham. In 1968 mains electricity came to the village, to replace an old world of log fires and paraffin lamps. To this day there is no mains

Rhanc y Mynydd

water to the village and every house makes use of a private or shared natural spring. Over the years, several homes have been made amongst the ruins of Rhanc y Mynydd, and I was told that, at one time during renovation, ashes could still be found in the empty fireplaces. More recently, I have noticed an iron bed-frame sticking out from the rubble.

It is amazing the speed at which a building up here can fall into disrepair. Take for instance Glan y Nant, or Bryn Goleu; barely 100 years have passed and already their shells have faded back into the landscape, their occupants but a memory to a generation that will take those memories to the grave, and who will survive to tell their stories then?

The ruins of Rhanc y Mynydd, 1960

Dylife Post Office. From left to right: John Lloyd the blacksmith (the smithy was next door), Jane Jones, William Pryce Evans, and the postman

Dylife School

This school was built in 1857, and was used for 68 years before being closed in 1925, due to decline in the local population. The school stood empty for many years before being demolished in 1941. The following is a school attendance list for 1921:

William D Williams	Dyfngwm Isaf	4/5/1908
Eirwen Williams	Bryn Eglwys	18/2/1908
Edward I Morgan	Rydd y Porthmyn	4/10/1908
Evan J Hughes	Bugeilyn	12/12/1908
Stanley Griffith	Rhanc y Mynydd	29/12/1908
Edith M Williams	Bryn Moel	17/6/1912
John H Morgan	Rydd y Porthmyn	12/6/1913
Arthur Hughes	Bugeilyn	15/7/1913
Rhydwen Davies	Rydwen	12/11/1913
Ifor T Jones	Tŷ Newydd	19/4/1914
Thomas P Wilson	Bronllys	6/8/1914
Mary M Jones	Tirpeg	18/12/1914

Later, there were more young children attending :

Gwen M Williams	Rydd y Porthmyn	13/8/1917
Tegwyn P Wilson	Blaen Twymyn	?
William Humphries	Tŷ Newydd	?
Pryce W Williams	Rydd y Porthmyn	?
Thomas Richards	Rhanc y Mynydd	?
Hannah Richards	Rhanc y Mynydd	?
Dewi Richards	Rhanc y Mynydd	?
Ireni Jones	Rhanc y Mynydd	?

After the school closed in 1925, the children were without schooling for quite a while, until they were told they would have to attend the school at Staylittle, a three-mile walk.

The school

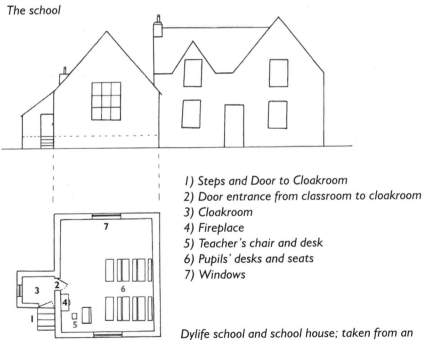

1) Steps and Door to Cloakroom
2) Door entrance from classroom to cloakroom
3) Cloakroom
4) Fireplace
5) Teacher's chair and desk
6) Pupils' desks and seats
7) Windows

Dylife school and school house; taken from an
original drawing by the the late T. P. Wilson

During one of my many visits to Powys County Archives Office, I was able to see the log book for Dylife school. The logbook is in hard back and quite extensive, covering in diary form the years from 1871 up to 1910. Below are some of the entries that I found to be of interest during my visit in February 2002.

Week ending Oct 27, 1871
Summary of the Government Inspector's report and remarks (If any) to be made.
'This is an efficient school. A map of the world is needed. H.M Inspectors states that a proper log book has not been provided by the managers. My lords, trusts that this deficiency will be Immediately supplied.

(Articles 34-40)   David William
(Manager)

April 21-25/1872
The attendance was very good throughout the week. On Monday night one of the school windows was broken by Hannah Davies and Catherine Hughes.

Inspectors Report 1873
Considering that this is a thoroughly Welsh parish the reading is good and the writing is fair. The arithmetic throughout the school is very defective. The children are much too talkative and the discipline is very Imperfect. The necessary offices are as yet Incomplete. A blackboard and ball frame are needed. My lords have ordered the grant to be reduced by one tenth under article 32 for defective Instruction in arithmetic.

The issue of a certificate to the teacher must be deferred until better results are obtained in this subject.

Day of Inspection May 7th 1873
H.M. Inspector – Myers

Manager – The Rev W Jenkins
Teacher – R.H. Williams

May 1st 1882
Commenced to mark the new registrars this morning.

May 4th 1882
Stopped five children to come to school this morning on account of the scarlet fever being in their homes.

July 1st 1887
Attendance very low on account of the children being busy with the "Peat".

July 15th 1887
Attendance much better this week owing to the peat season almost over.

May 4th 1889
Lost two boys this week owing to their parents leaving the neighbourhood.

Feb 10th 1890
Poor attendance this week due to the influenza epidemic that is sweeping the country, the master is ill.

Feb 28th 1890
Attendance is improving.
Oct 25th 1901
Drawing for the boys in the afternoon, sewing and knitting for the girls, average attendance for the week 26.2.

Dylife school, 1905

Feb 10th 1902
A visit of Inspection was paid to Dylife National School
on Friday 24th Jan 1902. The following defects in
connection with the premises were observed:

1/ The walls of the school are very damp in several
places and the room is in consequence very injurious to
the health of the pupils and the mistress.

2/ The ventilation is unsatisfactory.

3/ The room is not properly cleaned and dusted.

4/ The grate is not protected by a fireguard.

5/ The door of the boys' offices together with the
frame is out of place.

6/ There are no holes for holding ink wells in some of
the desks.

Feb 24th 1902
Fire guard used for first time. A lot of material arrived at Llanbrynmair railway station. Impossible to get to them from here as the farmers are too busy to spare time for the journey.

Feb 28th 1902
Materials arrived.

March 18th 1903
School chimney went on fire today, the room is very Smokey

Sept 1903
Arrived back from summer holidays during which time the school was whitewashed. The schoolroom is quite Smokey.

NOTES

It came to my attention that the schoolroom being 'quite Smokey' was a regular occurrence and there are several references to the need for windows to be left open all day as a consequence. Towards the end of the log book, increasingly, references can be found to children leaving the school due to their parents leaving the neighbourhood. This is almost certainly, in most cases, a result of the gradual decline of the lead industry in the area.

The master of the school in the 1880s was a Mr John Jones, who died, aged 55, in September 1888. His grave can be found in the churchyard. In the 1920s, there was a Village Shop somewhere near the School. A lady called Anne Roberts ran it, and among other things sold were flour, sugar, tea and sweets.

The Plas – Bugeilyn

Despite its size, surprisingly few details of the Plas survive. It was a large building, comprising 5 bedrooms upstairs, 3 bathrooms, each containing a wooden bath, and 4 rooms downstairs with a big kitchen. On the north end of the house there was a Keeper's Cottage, which had 2 rooms upstairs and 3 rooms downstairs, one of which was a boiler room, which provided the heating via a series of pipes laid throughout the house. Every door had strips of felt around it to stop the draught. There was also a garage with space for 2 cars, with a large room above with lots of hooks for hanging the grouse. Lighting was achieved, as with everywhere else, with paraffin lamps (lit with tapers made from rushes dipped in wax). One of the gamekeepers, around 1915, was Owen Hughes of nearby Bugeilyn farmhouse. Owen was also a shepherd and lived there with his wife, Hannah Jane Hughes. They raised 4 children,

The Plas, Bugeilyn, with the farmhouse in the background. 1968

Margaret, Evan John, Arthur and Gwen. Gwen relates that they had 2 cows, 1 horse and 2 pigs, and that all the cooking was done on a peat fire. Whilst the Plas was being built, two carpenters, formerly employed at Nant Ddu mine, who were working on the project, were lodging at Bugeilyn farmhouse and, as a thank you, they made a bench and a table for Mr and Mrs Hughes. Removed from the ruins by my father in the 1980s and restored, the bench now takes pride of place next to the fireplace at Belan. The Plas continued to be visited for shooting and fishing excursions up to 1932, when, for whatever reason, it was abandoned. It stood empty for many years, local farmers favouring it at shearing time because it could hold up to 700 sheep, although, by 1984, the building was so badly deteriorated that it was unsafe and was pulled down to make way for the more modern sheep sheds that are there today. Sadly, over the years, Bugeilyn farmhouse has also become a ruin. The whole area is now uninhabited right down as far as Ponterwyd, the odd scattered ruin bearing testimony to a way of life we today can only imagine.

3. The Three Chapels and St David's Church

The following is largely made up from notes passed to me, which were made many years ago by the late Will Richards.

Rydwen Methodist Chapel

Rydwen Methodist, also named Nebo Rydwen chapel, was run in conjunction with the Graig chapel, Staylittle. It was built in 1841, and opened in 1842 with a congregation of 60. When the mines were at their peak of production, as many as 100 formed the congregation. This was the first chapel to be built at Dylife; at the time there were 200 men working the Llechwedd Ddu and Esgairgaled lodes, with the population increasing rapidly alongside the growth of the mine. The following were Deacons at Rydwen, although at what point in the chapel's history I do not know.

John Lloyd, the Plas	Richard Evans, Blaen Twymyn
Alfred Evans, Rhanc y Mynydd	Edward Morgan, Top y Cae
Pryce Wilson, Bronllys	Richard Williams, Bryn Moel
John Richards, Tŷ Capel	David James, the Vicarage

I am informed by Will Richards that the last but one leader of the singing was a Mr William Williams of Bryn Eglwys, and the last was Bronwen Owen of Rydwen. By 1966, the congregation at the chapel was down to only 10 and, in 1966, the Chapel was closed; it was sold the following year. The chapel, now converted to a house, still stands today.

Seion Baptist Chapel

Capel Seion Baptist Chapel before renovation

This chapel was about 300 yards below the Methodist chapel and was built in 1852. Will Richards relates that there was a well for baptisms, although it was never used. Baptisms took place in a pool made at Nant y Maes. Inside the chapel there was seating for 150 people. Some of the following were deacons at one time or another:

David Jones, Ryd y Porthmyn
Margeret Evans, Rhanc y Mynydd
John Morgan, Rydwen

Richard Morris, Bryn Eglwys
Evan Davies, Star Inn

The last person to be a deacon at this chapel was a Mr Ellis Gittings of Bugeilyn. From 1900 onwards, the population dwindled, and by 1948 there was only a small number of members left, forcing the chapel to close in 1950. This chapel was run in conjunction with Staylittle Baptist chapel. 1n 1970 the chapel was standing empty, although it has since then been converted into a dwelling house.

Capel Coed

Capel Coed means timber chapel and was probably just that. It was an old storage shed for the copper, which stood at the Flourin and was given to the Independents by a Captain Garside, to equip and use as a chapel. This chapel was run in conjunction with Aberhosan chapel, five miles away. I have been told that in the cemetery surrounding the chapel in Aberhosan, headstones can be seen that can be attributed to miners bought down from Flintshire, who worked at Dylife. Capel Coed possessed a pipe organ, something the other two chapels in Dylife did not have. I am told the Minister of this chapel walked between the two chapels for years, through all weather conditions. He must have negotiated the steep path up the side of Moel Fadian and across the Glaslyn moor, an unenviable task, knowing how fast and impenetrable the mist can be, when it descends up there. During the chapel's history the following people were deacons at some time or another:

Dafydd Griffith, Dyfngwm Isaf
Griffith Wilson, Droppings

A Mr Thomas Jones was also a deacon at one time, but he emigrated to Patagonia. It is almost certain that Capel Coed was the chapel that the women and children of the village tore down and burned before Sir Watkin's men could dismantle it.

St David's Church

In days gone by, Dylife village could be divided in two, the upper part and the lower part, with St David's church in the centre, opposite the Flourin, where the minerals were crushed and separated. The church was built in 1854 and opened in 1856. It was on the 28th of April 1856 that the 'Ecclesiastical district of Dylife was formed for the spiritual accommodation of its Inhabitants'. The land for the church was given by the lord of the manor, Sir Watkin W Wynne, and included the site for the cemetery, which surrounds the church. It is likely that the cost of erecting the church was shared between Sir Watkin and the company running the mine at that time, although Will Richards remembers seeing inside the church a notice board with the following message:

> Incorporated Church Building Authority granted £140 towards building this church on condition that 207 seats are to be reserved free for the poorer Inhabitants of this parish.

The first vicar was a Rev. David Davies of Llangurig; one of his first tasks was to endeavour to provide education for the children of the village, and he succeeded in this in 1857, when a school was built at a cost of £250, the site again being given by Sir Watkin. The vicar's second self-imposed task was to press for a vicarage to be built. In 1859, in the upper part of the village, a vicarage was built. Nowadays, this building still stands as a dwelling, although it has been renamed Esgairgaled.

An interesting story to relate from 1860 was that the Rev. Davies had prepared eleven of the young people who worked on the washing floors for Confirmation by the Bishop, but the head dresser, a Nonconformist, would not let any of them go, under pain of dismissal. (C. J. Williams)

I am informed that seven vicars served at intervals, between 1856 and 1922. During a fierce storm in March 1908, the west end wall of the church collapsed, along with the bell tower; it was

St David's Church

The Reverend Headley going to Llanbrynmair in his pony and trap

rebuilt by October of that same year but the pipe organ was sold, as it had deteriorated badly. The first christening at St David's was of Sarah Ann Edwards in 1856, and the last was a Nona Williams of Plas y Llyn (otherwise known as Ryd y Porthmyn) in 1926.

Over the course of the years, St David's church fell into a state of decay and, in 1961, the Church Authority decided that the building would have to be taken down. In July of 1962 demolition work began and, by the end of October of that same year, the church had been razed to within a few feet of the ground. At some point, before the church was demolished, someone took the church bell and, to this day, the identity of the perpetrator remains a mystery. The first marriage at St David's was on September 27th, 1856 and the last in June 1915. Nowadays, the bare grass-grown foundations of the church can still be seen, as sheep pick their way amongst the decaying gravestones, and when the wind is still, there is a silence out of which a deep peace is born. One particular gravestone that day caught my eye and made me feel sad:

In Memory Of
Catherine, youngest daughter of
J.P. Hughes
Clerk to the Dylife Mines Company
By Mary Ann his wife
Obint the 26 day of January 1857
Aged 7 years and 3 months

A church Sunday School class

March 1908. West end wall collapsed. It was rebuilt by October, but the pipe organ was removed

There are many unmarked graves in the churchyard; in those days, a headstone was a luxury available to a few, and we can only wonder who lie in these silent graves, and what they did.

Will Richards saw at Machynlleth a register of marriages carried out at the church between 1856 and 1915. The following is a list of some of them:

Date	Name	From	Age	Occupation
27 Sept 1856	Richard Hughes	Rhiwdefeitty	27	Miner
	Mary Evans	Trannon		Farmer
Oct 1856	Peter Jones	Pennfforddgerrig		Miner
	Elizabeth Williams	Maes		
Oct 1856	Edward Roberts	RhancyMynydd		Miner
	Mary James	Pantyffynon		Farmer
May 1857	John Edwards	Nantyrhafod	22	
	Mary Richards	Nantyrhafod	23	Servant
Mar 1859	William Emanuel	Glannant	25	Engineer
	Mary Bonsal	Llywnygog	23	Servant
30 Sept 1859	Richard Morris	RhancyMynydd	25	Miner
	Hannah Davies		30	Dressmaker
16 Sept 1867	William Evans	Maes	22	Miner
	Margaret Evans	RhancyMynydd		

Date	Name	From	Age	Occupation
5 Nov 1870	Isaac Williams	Nant Ddu Mine	21	Mine Capt
	Catherine Jones	RhancyMynydd	19	
12 Dec 1870	Morris Jones	Bugeilyn		Miner
	Catherine Jones	Bugeilyn		
24 July 1875	Thomas Morgan	Maesmedrisol		
	Hannah Jones	Tŷ Newydd		
15 Dec 1879	Tudor Tudor	Tŷ Newydd		Farmer
	Jane Hughes	Vicarage	23	
1880	Thomas Jervis	Maesmedrisol		Farmer
	Ann Hughes	Penygraig		
26 Dec 1886	David Evans	Liverpool		Miner
	Ann Jones	Brynmoel		
Mar 9th	John Wigley	Rhosgoch	50	
	Mary Jones	Hirnant		
8 Apr 1892	John Richards		21	Miner
	Hannah Morris	Bryneglwys	27	
13 May 1896	John Smount	Carno	26	Blacksmith
	Mary Roberts	School House	23	
14 Apr 1897	Thomas Wickam	Newcastle on Tyne		Merchant
	Elizabeth Edwards	Vicarage		
9 Sept 1905	Thomas Hughes	Maesmedrisol	41	Labourer
	Margaret Jones	Pantyffynon	45	
1906	David James	Llanidloes	31	Cabinet Maker
	Catherine Roberts	School House	31	
5 Dec 1908	Levi Thomas	Penrhiwceiber	37	Miner
	Jane Evans	Post Office	40	
4 Oct 1909	John Tudor	Pennant Uchaf		
	Margaret Evans	Pennant Uchaf		
June 1915	Edward Howell Jones	Croeslynbach		
	Sarah Jane Richards	Bryngoleu		

St David's Church shortly before demolition, 1962

Demolition of St David's Church, September 1962

Demolition of St David's Church, September 1962

Bible from St David's Church

4. Siôn y Go

In the year 1725, a blacksmith by the name of Siôn Jones (John Jones in English) came to Dylife to work; he was from Ystumtuen, in Cardiganshire, where he had a wife and two children. After several weeks of hearing nothing from her husband, his wife set off for the mine to come and see him as she was worried. Bringing the two children, she made her way to Glan Dyfi, a village several miles south of Machynlleth and, from there she set off over the mountains to the works at Pen Dylife, a fair few miles distant. On reaching the works, the miners told her that Siôn was staying locally at Felin Newydd, and she and the children went there to meet him.

On their arrival, Siôn appeared pleased to see her, despite the fact he had been having an affair with a maid from nearby Llwyn y gog farm and, it is said, they were in love with each other and that is why he had not returned to Ystumtuen to see his wife.

After staying for several days, she and the children left for home, accompanied by Siôn. Where the road passed over Pen Dylife, Siôn murdered them, disposed of the bodies down a then disused shaft and returned to his accommodation at Felin Newydd. Everyone assumed his wife and children had returned to Ystumtuen.

Eleven weeks later, the Captain of the works sent some men to the shaft to recover some old timbers, and the bodies were discovered.

Siôn heard that the bodies had been found and, in a panic, ran

Castle Rock. The author, aged about 11, lends a fantastic sense of scale to the sheer size of the rock

Llyn Siôn y Go

up past Dyfngwm works, in the next valley, and, at a place known as Castle Rock, he attempted to throw himself off into a pool in the river Clywedog below. This pool was to become known as Llyn Siôn y Go.

The miners managed to stop him and he was taken to Welshpool, where he stood trial for the three murders, was found guilty, and the judge sentenced him to be hanged. He was then taken back to Dylife, where he was made to construct an iron frame in which he was to be hanged; this was to be his last job. A gallows was built at Pen y Crocbren, a stone's throw from the site of the old Roman Fort. He was fixed into the frame and set on horseback, the noose was placed around his neck, and the horse made to walk on.

As a warning to others, Siôn was left hanging for many years; I believe the gallows were taken down eventually, the timber post being used as a beam in one of the mine buildings. The cage with remains was thrown into the posthole.

In April 1938, having heard the local stories, Will Richards and Evan Gwilym Davies unearthed a skull and gibbet irons; this gruesome relic spent a while hanging in a shed at nearby Hirnant farm and, later, was put on display in a chemist's shop window in Machynlleth. The skull and gibbet are now on display at the National Museum of Wales at St Fagan's, near Cardiff. It is interesting to note that the site of the gallows is in the centre of a much older site, thought to be a burial mound. A report in the *Montgomeryshire Collection,* by W G Putnam, describes the mound as consisting of: '…a circular rock-cut ditch 56 ft in diameter overall, the ditch itself being 3 feet wide. The material from the ditch lies on its inner edge in a low bank 7ft wide.'

There is also an interesting story to relate that dates from the mid 1800s. It concerns a boy called Eifi from Pen Capel house, whose job it was to empty the Kibble at the top of Boundary Shaft (only a few hundred yards from the Gallows site). He claimed to have seen a headless apparition descending the ladders of the shaft; he ran home in a state of shock. For many years, too, the figure of a woman, thought to be the wife of the blacksmith, was frequently seen around, although it is said that she always disappeared when approached.

Whilst on the subject of the supernatural, in the comfort of the sitting room at Blaen Twymyn, Gwilam Wilson told me a story about the ghost of a miner who, it is said, was killed in an accident in Bradford's shaft. (So we can assume that this took place in the latter half of the 1800s.) The story goes that the body was brought to the surface and buried; however, the miner's clothes, being bloodied, were buried separately, in marshy ground known locally as Tŷ Maggi. I think this is on the bank below the Star Inn, about 100 yards to the south-east.

It was not long before the apparition of the miner began to appear regularly; eventually, one of the miner's friends summoned up the courage to approach the figure and ask what he wanted. The ghost said that his clothes must be dug up, and, then, he disappeared. As funny a request as this seemed, the wish was carried out and it is said that the miner's life savings were found in one of the pockets of his clothes. The ghost was never seen again.

Will Richards told my father a story, many years ago, of a miner who, at the start of his shift, was walking underground toward the shaft. In the darkness, lit only by candlelight, he was passed by three men who had finished their shift and were returning to the surface; he acknowledged them in Welsh and was surprised when they just seemed to ignore him completely. Puzzled, the miner made his way to the bottom of the workings, to begin his work. On arriving at the bottom level, he discovered that there had been a substantial roof collapse, and he raised the alarm immediately. Upon clearing the rock, the three bodies were found of the men the miner had seen walk past him earlier… Had it been the spirits of the men leaving the mine that the miner had seen?

I'm afraid I have no idea in which workings this is thought to have taken place, and it is always stories such as these that I try not to think too much about when venturing underground, as there is always a presence of some sort, and the uncertainty of what may be lurking in the darkness, just out of range of the torchlight. If I may quote David Bick:

"There is an aroused suspicion that we are intruders in a world of long departed souls, where with proper respect we ought not to remain for very long."

*The gruesome remains
of Siôn the Blacksmith*

5. Ffrwd Fawr

No book on Dylife would be complete without mention of the spectacular Dylife waterfall or Ffrwd Fawr. On the eastern side of Dylife, Afon Twymyn plunges one hundred and fifty feet into an area known as Ceunant Twymyn. This area comprises a two-kilometre-long section of the Twymyn Valley that is of exceptional geomorphological interest, as it provides a classic example of the process known as river capture, in which a former eastwards flowing tributary of the Afon Clywedog was diverted northwards, to follow the course of the modern

Dylife waterfall

Afon Twymyn.

A Site of Special Scientific Interest (SSSI) citation obtained from the Countryside Council for Wales reads:

> The Afon Twymyn at Ffrwd Fawr provides an excellent example of river capture in its headward reaches. Three kilometres from its source, the river falls fifty metres at Ffrwd Fawr and then enters a rejuvenated gorge section over a series of cascades and smaller waterfalls. The original course of the river lay eastwards to the Clywedog catchment but it was captured through headwater retreat of the Afon Twymyn, aided by structural and possibly glacial factors, leaving a dry gap as evidence of the diversion. Tributaries, which entered the Twymyn in the gorge section, have also been rejuvenated and there is active sediment supply to the river from adjacent slopes during extreme rainfall events.'

Pennant Valley

The whole area is an SSSI today and can best be seen from a viewpoint at the side of the mountain road, providing fantastic vistas through all of the seasons. I must advise that no attempt should be made to descend to the bottom of the waterfall. Over the years, there have been several accidents, some fatal. The waterfall can also be viewed from the footpath running along the top of the east side of the valley.

At the bottom of the Falls, carved into the rock, are initials reading WMR and EGD 1936. These initials stand for William Morris Richards and Evan Gwilym Davies, the two local men who dug up the gibbet at Penycrocbren.

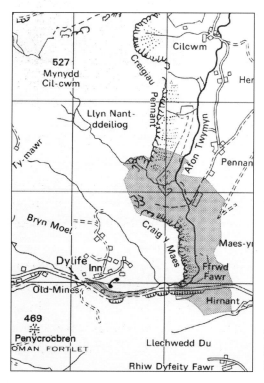

SSSI map – the shaded area is designated a site of Special Scientific Interest

6. Geological Report

The following is taken from a special report on the mineral resources of Great Britain, Volume XX, written by the late O. T. Jones, Professor of Geology and Mineralogy, Victoria University, Manchester. The report was originally published under the authority of His Majesty's Stationery Office in 1922 and was available at a price of 7 shillings.

Professor OT Jones

Dylife

(6-in. Sheet, Mont. 33 S.E., Long. 31° 40' 50", Lat. 52° 31' 55")

This mine lies in the centre of an elevated plateau about midway between Machynlleth and Llanidloes and on the old hill-road connecting these two places. The nearest station is Llanbrynmair, to which the distance by road is about 9 miles.

Three lodes have been worked and the workings on them appear to be in the main distinct. Unfortunately no plan is available and the information has been obtained verbally from miners who have worked in the mine. The main workings were on the Llechwedd Ddu lode, which dips to the north at about 75° to

80° and were carried on from two shafts. The Llechwedd Ddu or western shaft is situated in the valley opposite the row of cottages called Rhanc y Mynydd; it was sunk vertically to the lode for 50 fathoms and was then continued as an underlie shaft, to the 100-fm level. The Bradford or eastern shaft is 380 yards east–north-east, it was sunk to the 130-fm level and from this level a winze was carried to a further depth of 25 fathoms. The 120-fm level has been extended under the western shaft; towards the east the workings are said to reach about opposite the church, 300 yards east of the Bradford Shaft.

The western shaft is 50 yards to the west of a strong anticlinal axis which ranges north and south. The beds in the flank of the anticline dip at 35° to 40°. In the crest of the anticline and near the shaft a characteristic group of pale green mudstones is exposed, these lie in the lower part of the Frongoch formation and at a distance above the base which can be determined within narrow limits. It is probable that the Llechwedd Ddu shaft passed through this formation into the Gwestyn shales at a depth of about 80 fathoms. In the eastern or Bradford shaft those shales are probably at a depth of 150 fathoms, or approximately at the level of the winze from the bottom of the workings.

It is interesting to find that the debris lying on the surface near the eastern shaft, and apparently derived from the last workings, consist of the uppermost beds of the Gwestyn shales. Similar material near the western shaft is said to have come from the 90 fm level and thus agrees with the conclusion drawn from the examination of the surface. Another interesting feature is the occurrence of large calcareous nodules such as are commonly found in the association with the upper beds of the Gwestyn formation.

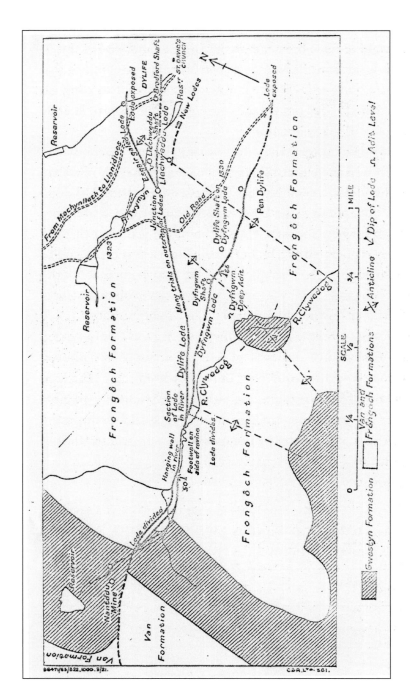

Geological map of Dylife and Dyfngwm districts

93

These are said to have been met in driving east and west at the 70 and 80 fm level from the western shaft. It appears therefore that the main ore body of Dylife lay in the lower part of the Frongoch beds and that the bottom of the mine coincides approximately with the base of that formation.

It is significant, too, that the workings were carried to a greater depth in the eastern shaft, where the Frongoch rocks are considerably deeper than they are in the western shaft. Although some ore appears to have been found within the underlying Gwestyn shales near the west end of the mine, it is clear that the bulk of it was obtained at a higher level. The richest ore is said to have occurred about half way between the two shafts at about the 40 fm level; the lode there was crossed by a soft joint dipping steeply to the west and was much enriched in its neighbourhood.

The workings on the northern or Pencerrig lode were carried out from a shaft sunk vertically to a depth of about 40 fathoms. This shaft is 200 yards north-west of the Bradford shaft. The lode is from 14 to 15 yards wide and although it yielded a payable amount of ore near the surface, the lower levels of the mine yielded blende only and the workings were not prosecuted further for this reason.

Output

In some years the returns for Dylife appear under Blaen Twymyn. Lead ore was returned in the years 1845-62, 1887-93, and 1899-1901. The greatest output was 2,571 tons in 1862.

Lead Ore	Lead	Ratio	Silver	Silver per ton of Ore	Silver per ton of lead
Tons 35,505	Tons 26,498	% 74.6	Oz 126,286	Oz 4.4	Oz 5.3

Blende – 391 tons.

Copper ore – 1,342 tons.

The amount of silver contained in the whole of the ore may be estimated at 154,160 oz.

Woodward Collection

An early mineral collector by the name of John Woodward, who collected minerals from several of the mid-Wales metal mines, visited Dylife around 1700. The following are examples he collected from 'Mr Harley's mine – Eskergalid'. Today they are housed along with many other samples in the Sedgwick Museum at the University of Cambridge.

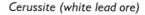

Cerussite (white lead ore)

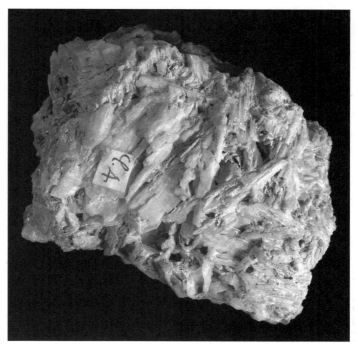

Cerussite and Anglesite

Bits of gravel, some striated, others not, but worn and round

Galena

Cerussite, found in Mr Harley's Mine, in a perpendicular fissure about 14 fathoms deep, amongst blue or Potters lead ore.

7. Dyfngwm

A Brief History

Whilst researching Dylife, I came across quite a lot of information about nearby Dyfngwm Mine. Although Dyfngwm never reached the notoriety or output of Dylife, it is certainly one of my favourite mines and well deserves a visit.

I found myself in the predicament of seeing that I do not have enough information to write another book, yet have too much just to allow it to sit on a shelf gathering dust. This brief history does not set out to be exhaustive but serves to put otherwise hidden material out into the public domain.

Lead mining at Dyfngwm dates back a long way, with the workings in the shadow of Castle Rock being even older. We know the Romans were busy in the area, and there is a level in the Clywedog Valley that Will Richards said the old miners attributed to them. There is also partial evidence in the immediate vicinity of the remains of hushing.

The workings lie on the southern branch of the Dylife / Dyfngwm lode belt. Working was originally effected from a shaft where the lode outcropped less than 250 yards from Dylife old engine shaft. Later, a deep adit was driven north from a ravine to the south, in the Clywedog Valley.

Mining was being carried out at Dyfngwm in 1725, when John the blacksmith was tried and hanged. Although no details have come to light, we can probably assume that the reference is to the

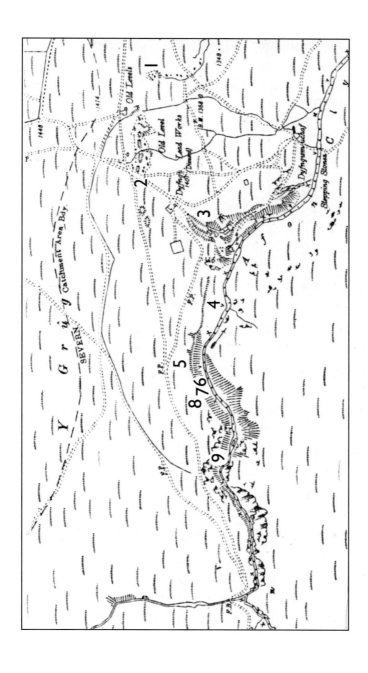

The workings at Dyffngwm. 1) Old Shallow Adit; 2) engine shaft; 3) Deep Adit; 4) Trial 1; 5) Trial 2;
6) Cyfartha Deep and Shallow Adits; 7) Roman level; 8) Trial 3; 9)Castle Rock

99

The immense tips dwarf the remains of the pumping wheelpit and crusher house. Much of this stone has originated from below adit level, and testifies to the extent of workings

workings on the outcrop of the lode near the Dylife boundary."

Dyfngwm was one of several mines to which a 31-years-lease was granted in 1771. Little is known about this period, although David Bick writes that, some years later, Dyfngwm was advertised as being 'now in profit', and came up for auction at the Spread Eagles in Machynlleth. Prior to this period, the mining sett was defined with banks (David Bick) and even today, some 200 years or so later, these boundary banks are quite visible in places.

In 1812, Dyfngwm was described by J Evans, author of *Beauties of England and Wales*, as '... being nearly worked out and having 9 shafts of about 14 yards deep belonging to a Mr Griffith Jones."

Mist rolls off the mountain with the remains of the 1800s crusher house in the foreground

I imagine the part of the sett described is that on the outcrop of the lode close to Pen Dylife. *Pigot's Directory*, which lists people living in and around the Machynlleth area for this period, also shows a Griffith Jones, lead merchant, at Dyfngwm in 1828.

In 1840, two miners on a three month tribute found an excellent course of ore soon after they started work. They engaged others to help them and raised enough ore to pay £400 in royalties to the Landowner, and to enable both men to buy themselves a fully stocked farm.

A vivid and detailed description of the mine around this period, although containing several inaccuracies, can be gained from this report written by the Cornish Mining Engineer, Mathew Francis, on 20 March 1847:

Dyfngwm Mine is situated near the summit of a ridge
of mountainous ground halfway between Machynlleth
and Llanidloes, the turnpike road passing within a few
paces of the sett and not more than 400 from the mine.
The district in which the grant is situated contains some
very large and productive mines, among which may
be reckoned Esgairgalid, Delive and Esgairhir. It is the
apex of the Snowdonian range and the veins are large
and well defined as they usually are in such districts. The
surface is principally covered with peat and lakes and
mountain brooks are numerously scattered along the
line of the hills, forming a valuable supply of water for
machinery. The mine is placed 200 feet above the level
of sea. The carriage of the produce is all down hill, the
shipping port being Derwen-Las on the River Dovey
three miles below Machynlleth, the price about 10s per
ton. The locality of Dyfngwm is immediately to the west
of Esgairgalid and Delive. The former in possession of
Messrs Pugh and Williams, yielding fair profits and the
latter an ancient mine which, from the evidence on the
surface, was formally largely productive. In Dyfngwm
mine the lode which has been recently attacked is
the Delive vein, it is about 4 fathoms to the south of
the Esgairgalid lode, which has not been seen in this
ground except on the surface, where it has been broken
through by the Dyfngwm adit mouth. The Delive lode
in Dyfngwm mine has been reached at a depth of about
40 fathoms below the surface of the adit level drawn
across the country to it, from a brook in the ravine to the
south of the lode (the surface portion of the vein having
been worked since time immemorial) at the depths of
40 fathoms from the surface where the lode has been for
some considerable distance to the east and west of the
crosscut, by the adit it seems to have yielded a great deal
of ore and in the 15 fm level under the adit driven some
40 fathoms east of the engine shaft, the backs yield in

places as much as 2 tons to the fm and westward, near the shaft, the vein is large and productive and the bottoms sink under this level some 40 or 50 fathoms west of the engine shaft, yield good steel grained ore. The 22 fm level has been driven about 30 fathoms east of the engine shaft and is under a winze nearly holed to it yielding about 1½ ton of ore to the fm and westward of the engine shaft the lode in this level yields some good ore to the north side of the working. I believe this 22 fm level, if driven westward, would go under some orey bottoms or underhand stopes before alluded to as containing steel grained ore. The Esgairgalid lode, as seen in Carfartha, is of immense width, say 30 foot rising up from the bed of the brook in great strength of crystalization and yielding some very fine ore. This lode might be crossed with a cover from 40 to 50 fathoms by driving Dyfngwm adit northwards 40 fathoms. In giving an opinion to the value of the sett, I rely with great confidence that this mine will eventually be found a great and profitable one. I consider that the average ground laid open by the level driven through it in the upper section of the sett will barely pay for working, the spots of ore, though good in some places, are not continuously so for any distance, but they afford evidence of a strong lode which I am of the opinion will be found changed with ore in depth much more solid on its nature and of much greater extent in its deposit and not withstanding the upper section of this lode is not so frought with solid ore, as I believe it will be found below nevertheless I should recommend that the Dyfngwm adit should be extended to it: because since it is so productive in Esgairgalid it is not improbable it will lay open profitable ore ground but also it will unwater the upper portion of the lode under afford facilities for the application of power for the systematic working of the mine. No great skill has been hitherto shown in the arrangement for mining the piece of ground. The wheel, which is an oak one, 40 ft diameter, 2 ft abreast, is placed in the ravine below the adit level, it draws a line of rods with a cambrious body and ill adjusted pit work. The line of rods it taken along the adit under a good light iron railroad, there is a small drawing machine attached to the rods to haul the stuff and a good 18 inch crushing mill attached to the wheel for reducing the ore, the wheel would have been much better situated on the dip of the hill near the back of the lode, where the stream might be conveyed and this arrangement would do away with great disadvantages as to drawing, wagoning, carriage and application to pit work, reducing a complex to a simple system. In order to lay open the mine fairly, an engine shaft should be sunk from the first surface as to command the two lodes at some considerable depth say 150 fathoms from the surface or 100 fathoms below the adit level, which with the proper application and machinery would cost about £5,000. Levels boldly extended from the shaft would lay open bodies of ore, which would leave very large profits. I would make an additional allowance for this, say 200 fathoms of level of £1,500, with a capital of say £7,000 and a well directed economic system of operation I have no doubt that Dyfngwm would become a large a profitable mine. I have studied the nature of such loads in positions similar to this of Dyfngwm and the examples I have read have lead me to the conclusion that although the lodes are large and coarse at the surface and the metals strongly smitten with blende and sulphur, yet in depth they become more purified and available for working and I feel no compunction or wavering in my mind on recommending the application of such or even greater than I have named for fairly developing resources of Dyfngwm mine. I rest satisfied that they will be found sufficient to repay the adventurers their outlay and so and leave a very handsome surplice for a long series of years.

In September of 1845, a lease of 50 years was granted to a new company, who, according to David Bick, comprised Edward Davies, George Hadley (acting as treasurer) and William Prosser. This trio had previously been much involved with the nearby mine at Rhoswydol

In 1847, the mine was under the supervision of John Reynolds, and had been for at least 5 years or so. He was responsible for overseeing the crushing mill erected in 1842. We know from the report that the main shaft was down to 40 fathoms below adit; a stope to the west, in the 22 fm level, proved to be ground worth £13 per fathom for lead, the lode at this point being 5ft wide. On August 16th, 1847, a discovery was made to the east, in the 22 fm level, from a winze sent down from the 16 fm level, proving ground worth £10 per fm. The men were set to strip the whole of the lode and soon opened 100 fathoms of good orey ground. In September, four bargains had been set in the 22 fm level and 2 in the 16 fm level.

In the month ending October 1847, 20 tons of lead were ready to ship and a further 20 unwashed. It quickly became apparent that, from the 22fm level downwards, the lode became richer. In the same month, Mr Reynolds wrote to the *Mining Journal*, 'The mine improves at every step the miners make daily, unfolding its wealth and assuring us of its extent and value.'

In 1848, the 40-ft wheel mentioned in Frances's report was still working the pumps and crushing the ore. There was a house for the manager as well as workshops for the smith and the carpenters. In this year, a report was made by Captain Edward Davies, It appeared that a winze sunk 6 fathoms below the 16 fathoms level, with levels driving east and west, would yield 15–20 tons of lead monthly. The lead could be mixed with black jack or blende, which at this time was readily saleable and used for repairing roads. It was also proposed to sink the engine shaft a further 30 fathoms and to drive an adit cross cut to the Esgairgalid lode. Captain Davies also observed that there were other parts of the sett that he considered worthy of trial.

An important management development at this time was the issue of 3,000 shares at a value of £10 each. 500 of these shares were to be sold and the money applied to the working of the mine, whilst 2,500 shares were retained and appropriated to the present adventurers in full payment for their expenditure on machinery and materials etc. David Bick writes, that this was a standard trick in the mining world; that having exaggerated the prospects at the mine, the shares would be advertised for disposal, to be sold, of course, by the promoters, i.e. Davies and friends, sadly the mine serving only as a means to an end.

In 1850 two new waterwheels were built, to power a six-headed stamp battery and a new drawing machine; the site was probably between the Afon Clywedog and the adit cross cut.

Various breakdowns and lack of results bought much criticism to Captain Davies, who had become manager by this time. However, by 1851, 60 men were employed, and 3 ft of nearly solid galena was discovered in the 32 fm level, whilst in the 42 fm level, the lode was found to be 15 ft wide of good orey ground, requiring twin levels to be driven side by side for stopeing.

In 1853, a road /incline was made down to the ore house by the main adit, allowing the ore to be transported out of the valley by cart. Previously, men carried the sacks out by hand and loaded the carts at the top of the hill.

It was decided to widen the adit in 1855, as there was a ridiculous arrangement in place, whereby the flat rods lay in a gully under the tramway, their efficiency greatly reduced by the debris of the years. Dry weather and frost also regularly interfered with the efficiency of waterpower, and Captain Davies set about making provision for a small steam engine to assist with the pumping.

Four weeks of drought in July 1855 were retarding the operations and, to make matters worse, a section of the works in the 60 fm level issued so much water that it was as much as could be done to keep the water out of the mine. However, by 2ⁿᵈ August, Captain Davies found it fit to write to the *Mining Journal*:

> We have rain sufficient to drown the mine. The ore begins to appear in the 60 fm level. The winze sunk from the 50 was nearly drained last night, I have let it to a party to sink through and others are driving under. This is very open ground otherwise the water would not have drained through so quickly, I shipped 10 tons of ore per the Bee.

By the 8ᵗʰ of September 1855, except for the occasional rain, there had not been enough water for mining purposes for eight months. Unable to pump the workings clear of water properly, the 60 fm level that was producing an average of 4 tons to the fathom had become flooded.

Dyfngwm had had to rely chiefly on its water reserve: a large reservoir, about a mile to the west, above the mine of Nant Ddu. With the water running so short and retarding operations, Captain Davies drafted all men on to widening the adit level, so as to enable it to be completed within a week. It was widened one foot, for a distance of 90 fathoms, 'The men breaking so much stuff that on some days it required 40 hands to tram the rock out.' Water was being collected in the reservoir, so as to provide for nine days pumping, should no further rain be had. The lead ore accounts for these past few months showed: August 17th, shipped per *Elizabeth and Mary* 21 tons; September 8th, shipped per *Propriety* 27 tons; making a total of 48 tons and a total of 41 tons dressed which would have been 50 had the water not failed.

As time went by, with no rain to speak of to turn the wheel, the water rose to within a few fathoms above the roof of the 10 fathom level. When the rain came in early October, Captain Davies reported to the *Mining Journal*:

> During the last week we had a fair supply of water, the rain increasing till yesterday when we got the first autumn floods. The water today is 24 ft below the 10. I never saw the machinery work so well or draw so much water as present: the wheel works 8 strokes per minute. Our heaviest work was in the 40 which is there driving double for a considerable length and the lode stoped for 15 ft in width. We will now lower the water below the 50 much better. Today some of our men can commence stopeing as the water clears from their bargains.

This rain was well received, as no lead had been dressed for 5 weeks. The ore dressers had been kept busy by re-dressing the waste and slimes. Also in this idle period, the tramway was removed from the main adit and re-laid in the new part of the level, giving the flatrods a separate and clear working compartment for themselves.

The foundations were being laid for a new engine house, the position of which had been approved by the engineers, and a tramway between there and the cart house was under construction, for the purpose of tramming materials. The settings for October

1855 were: The 60 east to 4 men to drive the level further. The 60 west to 6 men: ditto. 4 men to stope in the back. The 50 west to 6 men to drive the level further. The same level to stope in the back for 6 men.

Below the tips. A rusted and worn kibble guards the bottom entrance to the Dyfngwm gorge

By November, when a total of 29 men were employed underground, 30 tons of lead had been dressed, the larger part of it ready to be shipped by the *Prosperity*. Whilst the rain had impeded the masons working on the engine house, the large engine wheel, measuring 12 ft in diameter, for the steam engine had arrived at the mine, and all other materials for this project were on site, although, due to the weather, it was 1856 by the time the engine was up and running, and then, only 5 kibbles an hour could be raised until the new drawing machine arrived.

Around this time, workings at the west end of the 50 fm level had communicated with other workings at the west end of the sett (quite possibly the works at Cyfartha, 250 yds. or so distant). In June of 1856 the 60 fm east was still producing good ore, and a cargo of coal for the new engine was received at Derwenlas by the ship *The Dart*. The 70 fm level had also been reached at this point and by January 1857 the west level had still not entered a good bunch of ore, the lode being rather narrow and quite scattered. Winter had set in and, at one point, there was so much snow that it was blocking the flatrods; and the bad weather combined with the Christmas holidays bought the dressing of the ore to a complete stop. It was arranged that the trammers underground were picking the ore as it was mined, and throwing it on the stalls, so that, when the weather improved, the ore coming out would be much richer.

There had been a large amount of water in the 70 fm level since the 25th of December, and the pumps were barely managing to draw out a little more than was flowing into the mine. The weather continued to be frosty and snowy; the steam engine could not be used to its full advantage, for the fear of consuming all the coal before the new supply arrived. By using the wheel to draw from the 60 fm level, the mine was kept going enough to supply the dressing floors with a good supply of ore. A very important discovery of ore was made in the 60 west, producing upwards of 5 tons per fm in the richest parts. 4 fms of lode was stoped out and proved to be excellent.

Drawing was improved with the introduction of larger kibbles and a new chain, which enabled more ore to be bought out than previously. 27 tons of ore were shipped on *The Catherine and*

Margaret on the 29th December; 12 tons of ore was also shipped by *The Mermaid,* whilst 20 tons remained on the floors, awaiting shipment by *The Countess* when the carriers can get through the snow.

In September of 1857, Captain Davies found it worthy to praise his ore dressers 'For the manner in which they turned out their work.'

The total recorded returns for this year amounted to 376 tons.

Around 1858, a 36-inch condensing engine was acquired but, according to David Bick, for one reason or another, it is doubtful whether it ever arrived. In 1864, when work was down to the 82fm level, a twin 10-inch-cylinder horizontal engine (now 2 years old) assisted the pumping wheel in dry weather, working 7 and 8-inch pumps, whilst, in October of 1864, a steam traction engine arrived at the mine, having been driven all the way from Rochester, although this quickly proved to be a White Elephant. David Bick records that an ancient boiler that survives in a North Wales slate quarry may well be the remains of this engine.

An important discovery in 1865, on the Dylife / Dyfngwm lode in the Cyfartha level, provided sufficient backs above the adit level to give productive ground for years. Here, 2 adits and a winze have prosecuted the Dylife / Dyngwm lode.

By 1866, Captain Davies was coming under heavy and continued criticism. David Bick writes that a disgruntled shareholder accused Captain Davies of investing more time and effort in his farm at Dolcaradog, 5 miles away, than in matters of the mine. Davies was also accused of amassing large profits from questionable dealings in machinery; and that a clerk to the mine had to walk to work from

Machynlleth, although a house intended for Davies stood empty on site, as he preferred to live at his farm at Dolcaradog.

An article appeared in the *Mining Journal* of August 4[th.] 1866, in reply to a previous article sent in by Mr John Young ('Ex Officio'), who, according to David Bick, was once the chairman of the finance committee.

DYFNGWM MINE AND ITS MANAGEMENT

Sir – in your Notices to Correspondents there are almost weekly allusions made to Dyfngwm mine, and also mention made of, and remark on a printed letter by an 'Ex Officio'. On the face of your own remarks I presume you have pursued that letter. – You have however extra judicially delivered judgement against myself as manager. The question has been put on me why I allow these articles to appear weekly without being challenged? My answer is very simple and short. In the first place, I have attended during the last two years almost every general meeting of the shareholders. During the past 3 mths I have attended 3 such, at which the business of the mine was fully discussed. The usual way is for such matters as 'Ex Officio's' charges to be bought forward in person at such meetings. He was not present at one, and the shareholders, therefore and for other reasons, satisfactory to themselves, refused to discuss the subject matter of 'Ex Officio's' letters. Furthermore, at the last meeting permission to reply to these letters was refused to me. So long, therefore, as I remain an officer of the company my hands are tied, and this short communication is addressed to yourself. In reading 'Ex Officio's' letter did you put the question – to yourself of course – whether the contents were true or not? I have no hesitation in saying the greater part is not true. Such being the case I put it to your spirit of candour whether you are justified in permitting yourself being made the vehicle of these attacks, especially when I am precluded by Superiors from defending myself. I take this opportunity publicly thanking those able men, who quite unconnected with me or the mine, have kindly volunteered their services in my defence. At the present time I shall not avail myself of them. I shall, however at the proper time take my own course in my own defence. When I consider the means at my disposal, the difficulties I have connected with and the extraordinary mining times we are going through, I have not the least reluctance in subscribing myself in full.

Edward Davies
Manager of Dyfngwm Mine

On the 13th September 1866, the lode at the west end of the 82 fm level was not yielding more than one ton per fathom, and much of the 70 fm level had run in, due to poor timbering. The main shaft needed repair in several places and, despite the extent of the workings, no plans existed. By the spring of 1867, the miners had not received any pay for four months and although £52,000 had been earned from the sale of lead over the past sixteen years, hardly a dividend had been paid. Matters could not continue as they were and, with a lack of capital to invest in bringing the mine up to scratch, combined with the loss of faith in Captain Davies, there was not much hope for recovery; also, the Crown Inspector of Fisheries reported that the slime pits were constantly overflowing and there was no sign of any vegetation in the river, or on its banks, for at least 5 miles downstream of the mine. The mine was put up for auction at the end of 1867. Captain Davies eventually emigrated to America in 1871, although he returned to Wales and spent the rest of his life as a politician. He died in 1903.

The mine was to pass into the hands of a German company, under the directorship of a Colonel F P Stronsberg, a wealthy, slightly eccentric man, who seemed to treat the venture as an exercise in good mining. All the work seems to have been carried out to a rigid plan, ensuring that the underground workings were beautifully laid out. The only ore that seemed to be raised at this time was that necessary to prove the reserves in the mine. The shaft was re-timbered and new winding gear installed. One waterwheel did the pumping, whilst another worked the dressing floors. The horizontal steam engine still provided stand-by power when water was in short supply. In the summer of 1868, the 40 fm level communicated with the 30 fm level at Dylife, which made it possible to walk underground from one valley to the other, as well as greatly facilitating ventilation. There was also a house for the manager, and three to four more houses were built close to the mine, although they were never occupied as the company left in 1870, owing to the Franco-German war. At some point during his involvement with Dyfngwm, I believe Colonel Stronsberg was offered £10,000 for the mine, but refused to accept it.

The following is a report obtained from the late Will Richards, and made by Edward Hughes and John Jones, who worked in the mine when Colonel Stronsberg was the owner. John Jones was a very able mining engineer and, years ago, he was responsible for sinking pits at the South Wales Coalfields. Will Richards relates how, during the 1914 / 1918 war, John Jones went to be manager of the Nant Iago lead mine, under the shadow of Plynlimon. The report was originally in Welsh and has been translated into English:

DYFNGWM MINE REPORT

100 fathom level

This level has been driven 20 yards but no stopes have been raised, the work was abandoned before stopeing was commenced. There is good lead in this level.

90 fathom level

We do not remember the length of this level, but it was driven some scores of yards and has been stoped. The lode in this level parted in two and was crossed in the heading and good lead was found there, but no stopes have been raised in the cross cut.

80 fathom level

This level was driven a good distance but lost the lode, it was driven 50 yards without finding any lead. In Captain Nabieth and Sander's time, men were employed to cross into the heading and they came upon the lead within a few feet of the first level. There is about four inches of lead upon the face of the level and there is about a foot and a half of good lead in a mixture all along the level for the 60 yards that has been driven, this has not been stoped. In the bottom of this level a winze has been sunk to meet the 90 fm level but the 90 fm level is a good distance further back than the winze. There is about 18 inches of lead at the bottom of the winze.

70 fathom level

This level has not been driven as far as the lead in the 80 fm level, but we are confident that the lead in the 80 fm is going up to the surface, and there is fresh ground that has never been tested before crossing to the 80 fm level.

Surprisingly, it appears that Dyfngwm was then idle for a period of about 60 years. In 1931, Hirnant Minerals, who had previously worked the tips at Dylife, bought the mine from Mrs Jones, Tŷ Gwyn Farm, Aberhosan, for the sum of about £3,000 (W. Richards). The new owner was a Mr John Stevens of Brierley Hill, Birmingham, and no time was wasted in bringing the mine up to scratch, Dyfngwm was a much larger project than Dylife and much preparation had to be done to obtain access down into the deep valley and to lay out the site for the plant. Roads were repaired and new buildings erected. On 20th April 1931, the old pumping equipment in the main shaft was dismantled. It comprised of twin angle bobs, one inverted for twin pumps.

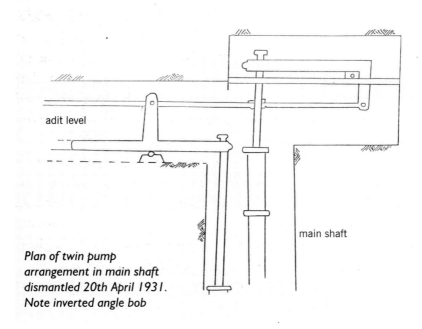

adit level

main shaft

Plan of twin pump arrangement in main shaft dismantled 20th April 1931. Note inverted angle bob

A new tram road was laid in the adit level, out to a fine new concentrating plant. The plant consisted of a hopper for the undressed ore at an upper level feeding a Blake stonebreaker, and descending in steps to a small granulator, Broadbent Rolls Mill, Pegson vibrating screens, a Ware Jig, two Hartz Jigs of two compartments each, and a large Ball mill, and four Overstrom vibrating tables, and at the bottom of the plant there was a shed where the dressed ore was stored in Hessian sacks to await carriage to Llanbrynmair Station by lorry, for onward transportation by train to Newcastle-upon-Tyne.

All this dressing machinery was driven by a 45-horsepower Blackstone diesel engine that had been hauled over the hill from Dylife, undoubtedly, not an easy task, since it necessitated negotiating the Camdwr road, which had only a gravel surface. The waste slime, an after-product of the dressing processes, was pumped over the river to the other side of the valley, to a height of about 30 ft, before it flowed on in a leat to filter beds further down the valley. Will Richards relates that the river remained unpolluted during the whole time the works were in operation; there were even fish below the filter beds.

Outside the main adit, a shed was erected, which housed a Petter's 100-horsepower twin vertical cylinder diesel engine. This engine drove two Ingasol air compressors, which worked two air hoists, one of which was at the top of the incline, to haul the trams, whilst the other was underground, at the top of the shaft. The compressors also provided air to work the boring drills in the main shaft, also the new pump, which was made by Evans and Tonkins of Wolverhampton. The pump was slung by a huge chain,

1935 Hirnant Minerals Dressing Plant

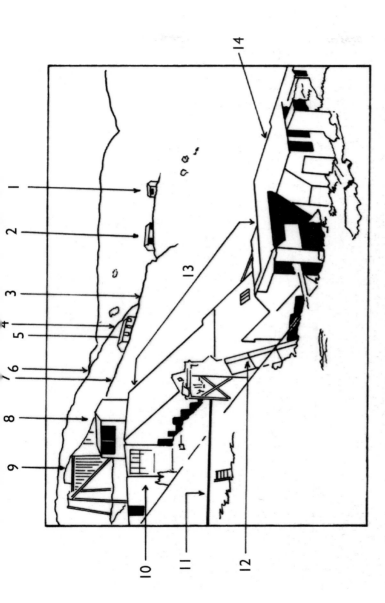

1) Manager's office; 2) Petters 100 HP diesel engine and two Ingersol Rand Compressors; 3) Tram line from shaft via adit;
4) Tram line up incline (also powder house); 5) Blacksmith and engineer's workshop; 6) Winding hoist at top of incline; 7)
Timber viaduct; 8) Blake stonebreaker; 9) Feed hopper; 10) Blackstone 45 HP diesel engine powering concentrating plant;
11) Tram line to clear waste and bring ore down from Cyfartha Cutting; 12) Conveyor; 13) Small granulator, Broadbent
Rolls mill, Pegson Vibrating Screens, Ware Gig, also two hartz figs of two compartments each and a large Ball Mill: 14) Four
Overstrom vibrating tables

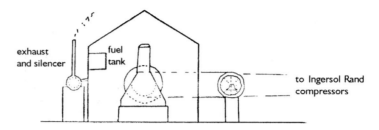

Cross section of Petter Engine Shed

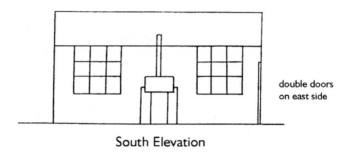

South Elevation

double doors
on east side

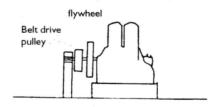

Vague idea of Petter 100HP (1931 Yeovil)
twin vertical cylinder engine

Sketches based on originals by Thomas Pryce Wilson

Powder house
(built of brick)

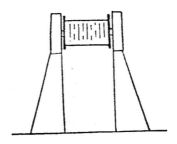

hoist at top of incline
for smaller loads

Mine tram
(side tipping for feeding hopper)

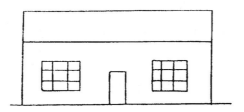

Blacksmith's shed

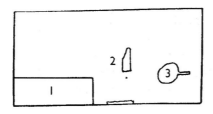

1) workbench; 2) anvil; 3) portable forge,
hand-operated fan by turning a handle

allowing the pump to be lowered as the water-level fell.

A lot of time was spent re-timbering the shaft with pitch pine and having the water pumped out, eventually down to the 40 fm level. The new company was eager to reach the 70 fm level, which was said to be very rich in lead ore.

The mine manager was a Mr G. F. Wallace, who had also managed the Hirnant Mineral plant at Dylife, but after his wife died, he was a broken man, and it was not long before he moved away. He was to be replaced by a Mr John Mitchell, a totally different person, '... rather bombastic and full of his own self importance.'

Most of the lead was obtained from the upper levels; these were very rich in zinc but much of it was left uncut within the levels as there was no market for it, although some of it was dressed, and, to this day, several rotting Hessian sacks containing zinc can be seen at the foot of the dressing floors.

I was lucky enough to know the late Thomas Pryce Wilson, Assistant Engineer at Dyfngwm mine from 1931–1935. This following excerpt from a letter he wrote to me provides a fascinating insight into life at the mine and its day to day running:

On November 25th, 1931, I was offered my first employment as assistant to the engineer, a Mr Toy from Llanidloes, Mills Foundry who was in charge of erecting the plant. Although my wage was only 10/- a week I was as happy as a sand boy, and Mr Toy taught me a great deal about engineering. Within nine months I was on £1 weekly, the top paid miners were only on £2.10.0 weekly, there was only 12 of us working in Dyfngwm in September 1932, the number increased slightly later. After the plant was completed and running Mr Toy and I were on maintenance work and a little blacksmithing such

Thomas Pryce Wilson, Assistant Mine Engineer 1931–1935

as keeping the miner's boring drills sharpened etc.

I eventually was in charge of the two diesel oil engines also but once started and oil tanks filled would run for hours unattended.

I can't quite remember when the operation of pumping out the water from the old workings started. Then the Petter oil engine was run continuously night and day with Rhydwen Davies and I on alternate 12 hour shifts with another person in charge of the pump underground but neither needed much attention but was apt to freeze up and had to be thawed out. The descent down the shaft was by 14 ft long ladders and by the time the pumping operation was stopped, May 11th 1935, there were 22 ladders. It was not part of my duty to go down the shaft but did several times, it is debateable which is worse, staying outside on ones own or going down the ladders, both quite eerie. Pumping the water out from the old workings proved beyond the capacity of the pump and when I had gone home to Mountain Ash for a weeks holiday I received a telegram "no need to rush back

Thoms Pryce Wilson, Assistant Mine Engineer. Bandaged after breaking his finger in the winch at the top of the incline

mine closed down", this came as a great surprise to all of us (May 17th 1935).'

The mine was closed down owing to the death of Mr Stevens, the owner, whose widow decided to sell the mine. Mr John Mitchell, the manager, was kept on until 1936, looking after the mine but, with the low price of lead, no new company was formed and the mine remained unsold. Later in 1936, the mine was sold to Messrs. Thomas Ward, Sheffield, for dismantling, and all the machinery was sold or taken away to Briton Ferry as scrap. Will Richards and Edwin Davies stayed on to help with what must have been a heartbreaking task. Most of the buildings were sold to local people.

The recorded returns at Dyfngwm amounted to 4,930 tons of lead ore and 134 tons of copper ore, plus 74 tons of lead and 8 tons of zinc, from the time Hirnant Minerals were there.

Many surface features survive at Dyfngwm. Outside the deep adit, the foundations to the air compressor shed survive and the route of the tramline can be traced to the concrete foundations

70 years on, Thomas Pryce Wilson's grandson, Owen, stands at the site of the blacksmith's shed where his grandfather worked.

of the Hirnant Minerals dressing plant. Below the tips, the 1842 crusher house is visible and, above, the site of the pumping wheel. There is more than enough to keep the industrial archaeologist busy here, both above and below ground, separating the different eras of archaeology, some in places partially erasing that which went before. The mine is now a scheduled ancient monument and has also been recommended for scheduling as an SSSI (Special Site of Scientific Interest).

I found this fantastic example of a roller wheel close to the river in 2005 – interestingly, quite a distance from where most of the activity was centred.

Behind the Petters Engine Site, the deep adit can be seen with the early way for the flatrods above. The tram incline lies to the left

On the hillside east of the deep adit, a curious depression; a little way beyond, a vertical gash leads down the rock toward the site of the Petters Engine, whilst above, a leat winds down from the direction of the engine shaft. Obviously quite ancient, this area of the site needs more interpretation

The following is a wages bill for the fortnight ending 14.09.1932, when there were twelve people employed:

John Williams	Goginan	12 days	£5.0.0
David Williams	Goginan	12 days	£5.0.0
John Jones	Staylittle	12 days	£4.10.0
W Christian	Cardiganshire	12 days	£4.10.0
EG Davies	Rhydwen	12 days	£4.10.0
M Richards	Tŷ-Capel	12 days	£4.10.0
R Foulks	Staylittle	12 days	£5.8.0
S Wilson	Blaentwymyn	12 days	£3.18.0
Joseph Jones	Dolydd	12 days	£3.12.0
H Thomas	Staylittle	12 days	£3.12.0
J Jones (Junior)	Staylittle	12 days	£3.12.0
TP Wilson	Bronllys	12 days	£2.0.0
			£50.2.0
Insurance Stamps			£1.17.2
Lorry Garage			£0.4.0
TOTAL			£52.3.2

8. Waterpower and its Application

Water has been utilised for mining purposes for hundreds of years; originally it was used for ore dressing, washing and hushing, the latter a method of revealing the ore. Water would be gathered in a small pool, or dam, and then released, and the torrent would wash away the soil (or overburden) and expose the ore beneath. There is evidence that hushing has been carried out at Dylife, Dyfngwm, and at a number of other metal mines in mid Wales. (Fine examples of hushing, though not at Dylife or Dyfngwm, are given in David Bick's *The Old Metal Mines of mid Wales Part 6*.)

The abundance of water in these hilly areas led to it becoming the primary source of power. Waterwheels were used for many years, although it was not really until the 1800s that the use of the waterwheel became commonplace. Typically made of iron or wood, or both, the waterwheel had four main applications:

1.   Pumping
2.   Winding
3.   Crushing (Stamps or rolls)
4.   Ore dressing plant

Most waterwheels were overshot, as this was the most efficient way of applying water to the wheel, compared with an undershot, or a breast shot, wheel. For example, the overshot wheel needs only about a quarter of the volume of water required by an undershot wheel since it uses the weight of the water rather than just its impulse.

The drawing house for the Martha Wheel

Without dwelling on waterwheel mechanics for too long, it might be useful to explain that the main disadvantage with an overshot wheel was the need for constant adjustment of the water flow through the control gate. A decrease in water meant a decrease in load on the wheel, which could cause the wheel to speed up suddenly. This, understandably, is undesirable for pumping and winding applications, and it would be someone's job to attend to the wheel, to ensure that everything ran smoothly. In the 1870s, the job of controlling the Martha wheel and the Boundary shaft drawing machines at Dylife, was entrusted to a John Hughes, who resided at Esgairgaled.

We are all familiar with seeing the big cast iron pipes of rising mains, sticking out of a lot of the shafts in these mountains. But what of the other end, often many hundreds of feet below the surface, lost under thousands of gallons of water. The diagram below shows a typical arrangement. The bucket, or sinking lift as it is known, shows an egg-ended windbore (1) with a clack valve (2) within the working barrel (3). As the plunger descends, water is forced from the cistern through the clack valve and into the pump column. A succession of this plunger action draws water into and up the pump column. Each stroke of the pump carries up a quantity of water equal in volume to that displaced by the plunger pole

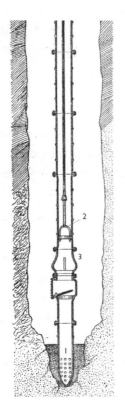

A clack valve found in the Llechwedd Ddu area, now at Llywernog Mining Museum. Peter Harvey informs me it has seen little if any use, and may have been a spare

David Bick records that 'Waterwheels driving reciprocating pumps required delicate adjustment, especially in conjunction with long runs of flat rods. Balance boxes were usually fitted at the shaft (to counteract the weight of the pump rods) and at the wheel itself.'

Overall efficiency was about 50%, leading to a simple formula thus: 2 x Height of pumping x outlet flow = Wheel diameter x Flow over wheel.

Drought and frost would have presented their own problems, sometimes bringing wheels to a standstill for weeks at a time.

In addition to this need for fine-tuning, it was absolutely essential to have a good and reliable fall of water. To provide this, several large reservoirs were built at Dylife, and one at Dyfngwm, totalling five in all, namely:

Rhyd y Porthmyn Pool

This reservoir was built in 1853 and must have dominated the landscape at the head of the Twymyn valley. Water was drawn off the lake by a sluice at the nearby cattle grid and conveyed to the Red Wheel via a long leat that ran below Rhanc y Mynydd, although the leat was later altered to run behind the houses, and was crossed by two footbridges.

Excess water was drawn off by means of a tunnel that runs right under the lake. The tunnel still exists today and runs for about 52 m, coming to a stop somewhere under the present shoreline. The tunnel is of a good size and masonry-lined; except for some deterioration at the entrance, the stonework is in good condition, and a little of the sluice mechanism is intact at the end of the passage.

Rhyd y Porthmyn Pool

The tunnel under Rhyd y Porthmyn lake

Following a fierce winter in 1968, part of the embankment collapsed and over half the lake emptied into the valley below. I am told no one was injured and no livestock lost, only the fence that crosses the brook at Glan y Nant was washed away. In March 1969, the fence was replaced and it lasted 35 years, before being renewed in 2004.

Remains of a sluice control at the end of the tunnel

Cwm yr Engine

These reservoirs were probably the first to be built in Dylife, and may date from as early as 1840. There is a chance that the lower reservoir may precede the upper pond in date, and the latter was an extension that was added when Llyn Nant Ddeiliog was built. It was a popular fishing haunt for those who knew about the lakes in the 1960s. Nowadays, only the upper pond contains water and, no doubt, a few fish. Below the embankment to the lower pond, a fine channel cut in the rock marks the position of the overflow, whilst an outlet pipe complete with sluice door can be seen in the stream.

The towering bank of the lower of the reservoirs at the head of Cwm yr Engine

Llyn Nant Ddeiliog

This reservoir was built about 1850, to the north of Dylife. A long leat brought water to the upper reservoir in the Engine Dingle. Not long after the 2nd World War, a scout, camping in the Pennant valley, walked up to the lake and went for a swim. Unfortunately, the boy was taken with cramp and drowned, and subsequently, the embankment to the reservoir was blasted with explosives. Today, the water content of this lake is a fraction of what it used to be. Provided you can swim, the reservoir is quite safe. I know of a local lady who takes her children there regularly in the summer months.

Llyn Nant Ddeiliog

Nant Ddu (Feeding Dyfngwm)

This reservoir was built, without permission of the landowner, Sir Watkin, in 1852, above the mine of Nant Ddu, to serve the waterwheels at Dyfngwm. The water, after leaving the reservoir, flowed down the brook known as Nant Ddu and into the Clywedog. In the upper part of the Clywedog valley, the river was tapped by a single leat that would take the water past castle rock, through an arch carved out of the rock, and down the valley to Dyfngwm. This is the only leat in the valley, and there is every chance that it tapped the Clywedog many years before the reservoir was built, and probably served the 40 ft oak wheel in 1847.

Interestingly, the mine at Nant Ddu (also known as Cyfartha), had a leat that tapped the brook within 50 yds of the reservoir,

Reservoir for Dyfngwm at Nant Ddu

taking off water to power a pumping wheel before flowing into a leat, and along an aqueduct, to the crushing wheel. It was then released back into the Nant Ddu, from whence it would make its way to Dyfngwm.

The reservoir probably continued to be used by the mine at Nant Ddu for several years after the start of the period when Dyfngwm was idle, following Colonel Strasberg's departure in 1870. The reservoir survived until 1960, when the landowner, a Mr Morris Griffith, set about draining it, by having a small section of the embankment by the sluice dug out. As soon as the water started to come through, the hole became larger. Today, an embankment and a few timbers (no doubt part of the sluice) are all that remain of the reservoir, the valley floor reverting back to the heather and boggy moor land it used to be, all those years ago.

The positioning of these reservoirs was quite important. As a general rule, they would utilise the natural lie of the land. Natural hollows, steep sided valleys, and naturally wet water catchment areas were all favourable, and any site smaller than one acre would be insufficient.

The reservoirs at Dylife and Dyfngwm were typical in construction. A large embankment made of earth and stone held back and contained the water, with a

Part of a Dyfngwm waterwheel found near the crusher house in 1989. Note the provision in the casting to accomodate the buckets

sluice mechanism installed to control the rate of outflow.

The water would flow to the wheels along man-made ditches, called leats. Cut by hand over miles of unforgiving moor land and, more often than not, through solid rock, these leats can be found just about everywhere in this area; tracking them to their source often makes for an enjoyable walk. At the end of the leat, the water would be conveyed over the wheel by a series of wooden troughs,

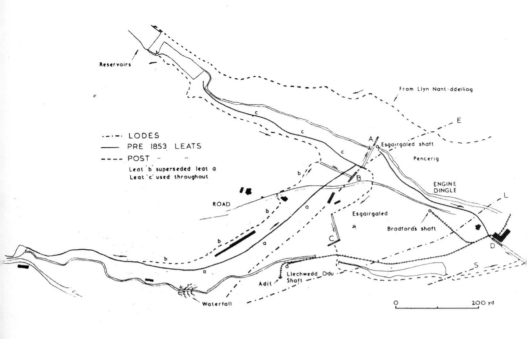

Lode outcrops and probable development of the watercourses,
as outlined by David Bick

A First site of Black Wheel (the pit partly survives) E Esgairgaled lode
B Second site of Black Wheel   L Llechwedd Ddu lode
C 63ft or Red Wheel (the pit survives)   S South lode, visible in stream
D 40ft crushing wheel

called launders; sometimes, a wooden aqueduct was necessary to
cross over buildings, or other features, such as a fall of ground.

David Bick's map is fairly comprehensive, as far as the
development of the water courses is concerned. However, over
the years, I have come across several more, which are detailed on
the opposite page.

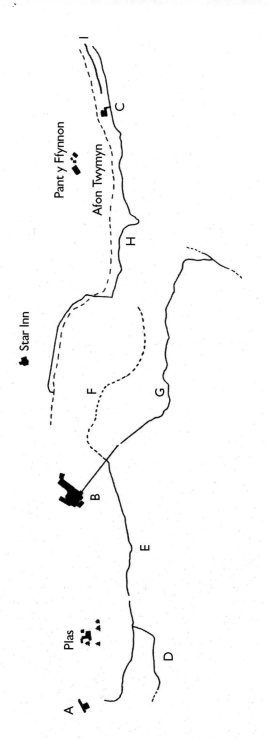

A   Red Wheel
B   40ft crushing wheel
C   50 x 6ft drawing wheel
D   Leat from Llechwedd Ddu
E   Leat from Red Wheel to 40ft wheel
F   Later extension to leat
G   Leat from valley to the east
H   Leat to 50 x 6ft wheel
I   Leat to filter beds

Castle Rock. Here the leat goes through the lode by means of a short tunnel

A section of the Dyfngwm leat cut through the solid rock. In the background, Castle Rock looms out of the gorge

Leat to the 50 x 6ft wheel

This leat dates from 1860 and, in its upper reaches, it has all but vanished. The leat starts on the north side of the river, about 60ft from the exit from the tunnel under the road, and it was fed by a big iron pipe that carried water from the dressing floors. It follows the fence line, running parallel to the stream, before crossing over by means of a wooden aqueduct below Bryn Goleu.

For about 100 yds, the leat becomes difficult to trace, as it has been buried by the tips from the Hirnant Minerals dressing plant above. However, the leat soon re-emerges and heads down the valley to the 50ft x 6ft wheel.

As a general rule, in the bottom of a wheel pit there is usually an arch, or some type of provision to allow the water to escape once it has passed over the wheel. Without a means of escape, the used water would fill the wheel pit and retard the efficiency of the wheel. As yet, I have not managed to find an exit from the 50ft x 6ft wheel pit, although there is an interesting channel cut into the rock on the side of the pit downstream of the drawing machine, I hardly think, however, that this was the exit for the water.

This leat does not stop at the wheel, but continues east for approximately 80 yards, the water is then discharged into another leat, about 30ft below. (I believe this leat also picked up the used water from the 50ft wheel, although haven't as yet worked out how). This lower leat then flowed down the valley and across the steep slope between the road and the waterfall, and terminated in a series of 6 settlement pools. The site of these pools can still be discerned, in the field just below and to the right of the Pennant view-point. From there, the water was released into a brook that allowed it to flow back into the Twymyn, just below the second waterfall.

This system was certainly active in 1886 and may date from the late 1860s. In 1863, there was nothing in place to filter the waste water, and the Dyfi Angling Club, whose members fished for salmon, complained that harm was being caused to their sport. In 1865, the matter was raised in Parliament and it was claimed that £50,000 loss of value was caused to the owners of land on the banks of the Dyfi by the refusal of the Dylife Mining Co to spend £500 on preventing pollution (C. J. Williams). Bright defended the company, saying he would be glad to spend the money to put an end to a nuisance that he himself believed to be grossly exaggerated. The position of the settlement pits can still be made out, although almost lost under a carpet of rushes; this area came to be known as Pant y Slime.

I will digress here, to talk briefly about pollution. Pollution is at least as much of a problem today as it was back in the 1800s. Due to a mine's basic need for water as a source of power, most mines are situated very close to one or more watercourses. The problem today with the legacy of abandoned mines is that, because of their proximity to watercourses, it doesn't take very long for high levels of lead, zinc or copper to enter the local streams and rivers. The effect these metals have is to raise the ph level of the water, making it more acidic and, because the surrounding rocks are devoid of carbonates to act as a buffer, the acidity will continue to rise, creating all sorts of environmental problems. In June 2002, Dylife was one of 50 mines earmarked for remediation.

The Dylife Waterfall area, 1886. Note the leat coming from the left, feeding the six filter beds before returning the water to Afon Twymyn

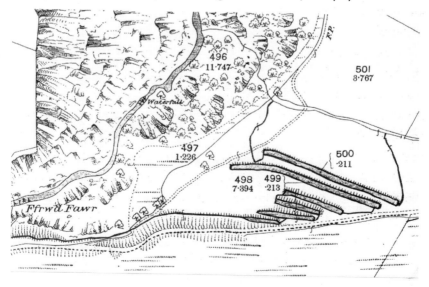

Remains of a sluice on a bank opposite the Star Inn

Leats opposite Star Inn

On the hillside opposite the Star Inn there is a leat, coming from the valley to the east, that winds its way across the hill towards the 40ft crushing wheel. It doesn't unite with the leat from the Martha wheel, as I originally thought, but discharges into a launder above that leat. This would explain the double launders that can be seen in the left of the picture on page 35. I am unable to attach a date to this leat, but it may have been an early leat to the dressing floors, perhaps predating the leat from the Martha wheel. An interesting, square, concrete sluice mechanism survives on the hill above the remains of the weighbridge. I also noticed traces of some kind of ancient ditch running almost parallel, further up the mountain. The leat to the 40ft crushing wheel had also been extended for quite a distance past the point where it discharged into the launders; the remains of a ditch can be traced from there to the roadside within 70m of the Hirnant Minerals dressing plant.

Leat in the Llechwedd Ddu area

This leat starts on the hillside south of Glan y Nant and makes its way across towards the workings at Llechwedd Ddu. I believe this section of the leat is quite old and, more than likely, finished in a hush on the Llechwedd Ddu lode below Alfred's shaft. From here, at a later date, the leat has been extended and continues east for a fair distance before dropping down to join the leat to the 40ft crushing wheel directly opposite the Plas.

Tunnels by the Dressing Floors

Although, strictly speaking, these are not leats, they deserve a few lines. The tunnel that runs under the road dates from at least the 1800s, maybe earlier. I believe it was driven for the purpose of providing a more convenient position for the stream, bearing in mind that the whole area in front of the school and St David's church is made up of mine waste.

The tunnel is cut through the solid rock for most of its length, apart from the northern end, which is stone lined where it passes beneath the tips. The exit from the tunnel used to be much larger but was modified by the council in the late 1990s, as the bank above was eroding.

Inside the tunnel, large, cast iron pipes kept the water from the dressing floors separate from the stream and conveyed it to the leat serving the 50ft x 6ft wheel. These pipes were removed for scrap in the Second World War, although one pipe was inaccessible and had to be left in the tunnel. It is worthy of note, that, as well as

Tunnel under road

the iron pipes, the large iron flywheel from the 20-inch engine, left behind when the engine was scrapped, was also taken for the war effort.

It is important to remember that the stream we see today in the dressing floor area was once largely under cover; the water was conveyed under the edge of the dressing floors through a masonry tunnel. On the south side of the stream and not far from the entrance to the tunnel under the road, part of this tunnel still exists, whilst on the opposite side of the stream, a large, wooden pipe sticks out from beneath the edge of the dressing floors.

Lastly, after carefully studying this area and closely scrutinising the map of 1886, I believe that the stream that flows down the Engine Dingle and under the present mountain road may not have

Inside the masonry tunnel that skirts the edge of the dressing floors

always followed that course. There is evidence to suggest that the original course of the stream lay to the east, right under the car park/gravel area, and emerged to the left of the exit, to join the tunnel under the road.

It is certainly something to think about, next time you are in the car park – is there a stone-lined tunnel, sealed at both ends, now quiet from the rush of water, some 30ft below your feet?

Waterpower was harnessed for applications other than mining. This wheel under restoration at Belan drove farming machinery in days gone by, and is one of only two in the immediate area that have survived into the present day

At rest and all but forgotten. This other wheel, in a shed at a farm in Aberhosan, served a similar purpose

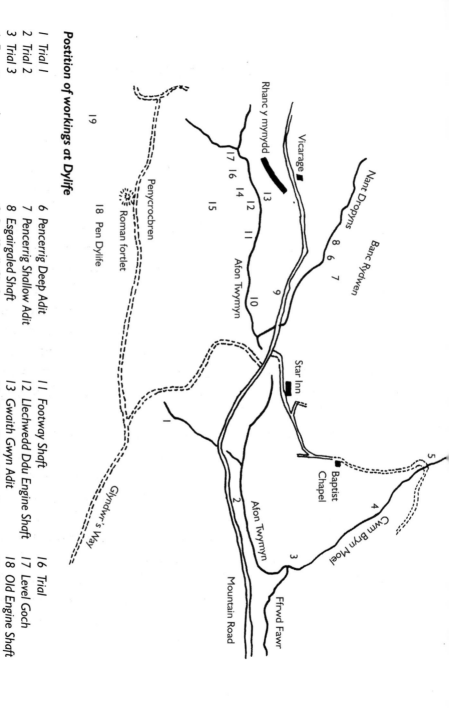

Postition of workings at Dylife

1 Trial 1	6 Pencerrig Deep Adit	11 Footway Shaft	16 Trial
2 Trial 2	7 Pencerrig Shallow Adit	12 Llechwedd Ddu Engine Shaft	17 Level Goch
3 Trial 3	8 Esgairgaled Shaft	13 Gwaith Gwyn Adit	18 Old Engine Shaft
4 Forgotten work	9 Bradford's Shaft	14 Great Dylife Adit	19 Boundary Shaft
5 Cwm Bryn Moel – trial	10 Shaft on South Lode	15 Alfred's Shaft	

Map labels:

Rhanc y mynydd
Vicarage
Nant Dropyns
Banc Rydwen
Penycrocbren
Roman fortlet
Afon Twymyn
Glyndŵr's Way
Star Inn
Baptist Chapel
Cwm Bryn Moel
Afon Twymyn
Mountain Road
Ffrwd Fawr
Pen Dylife

9. Underground Exploration Today

The aim of this section of the book is to provide the explorer and the industrial archaeologist with an insight into the workings at Dylife and Dyfngwm as they are today and is by no means meant to act as a guide. The sketch maps are not to scale, as I have included the relevant distances in the descriptions.

The workings at both mines are quite extensive and extend to a considerable depth. Whilst it is possible just to walk into some of the old levels, others should in no way be explored without the accompaniment of an experienced guide, as unstable rock and the unexpected pose an ever present threat. It is important always to treat workings of any nature, and any relics within, with the respect they deserve, and to remember the countryside saying: 'Take only photographs, leave only footprints.'

I have been venturing underground here since the age of 14, but I have re-surveyed all the workings in the last two years, to try to make the reports as accurate as possible. All the pictures are recent, as well, but it is important to remember that, from year to year, conditions underground can change considerably.

All the footpaths and rights of way can be identified from the Ordnance Survey map sheet 135, Scale 1:50 000, or sheet 215 of the O.S. Explorer series, Scale 1:25 000. The landowner's permission should always be sought before any excursions are undertaken. Last, but not least, I do not accept any responsibility whatsoever for anyone who chooses to venture underground, accompanied or otherwise.

Trial on the Dylife/Dyfngwm lode

Dylife

Dylife Trial 1

I found this adit on 5 September 2004, quite by chance, whilst I was tracing the origin of a leat on the bank opposite the Star Inn. The adit is situated on the south side of a small valley and very near the top; it is not easily visible, its entrance is shrouded by hanging vegetation and its tip completely grass-grown.

I could hardly contain my excitement at finding another previously undiscovered adit at so late a point in my research. It certainly proves the importance of going over old ground, especially at a site such as this, where there is always something new around the corner, waiting to be discovered.

Inside the adit, a tunnel of a decent size, quite narrow but with plenty of standing room, has been driven south for approximately 15 fathoms, in an obvious attempt to cut the Dylife lode, but no lode seems to have been found. Half way into the workings, a tunnel has been driven in a westerly direction for 10 fathoms and, again, no lode has been cut. The entrance to the adit leading to the junction within is about 3 feet deep in water and mud and there is a fair amount of loose rock inside.

Trial on Dylife lode

The date of the working is unknown, and it is not marked on the 1st edition O.S. map; there is every likelihood that it could date back to the 1700s. Just inside the adit, on the left, the rock has a natural, smooth, flat surface, possibly indicative of a natural joint that the miners exploited to make the driving of the tunnel easier.

Trial 2 on the Dylife lode. This goes right under the mountain road

Trial 2

This trial is about 400 yards upstream from the Dylife Waterfall and not far from the 50 ft waterwheel pit. It had been driven south for about 130 fathoms by a Captain Reynolds, in an attempt to find the Dylife / Dyfngwm lode; some sort of lode was found but whether it was the Dylife / Dyfngwm lode is uncertain. The tunnel is still accessible today and goes right under the existing mountain road, although it is knee-deep in water for the most of its length.

Trial 3 – Nant y Maes

This level was probably driven for the purpose of finding the Llechwedd Ddu lode, although no lode was found. The level is very old and is marked as an 'old level' on the first edition Ordnance Survey map of 1885. The entrance to the tunnel is partially collapsed and, inside, a tunnel has been driven west for about 5 fms, although it is much deteriorated, and chest-deep in water for at least half that distance.

Nant y Maes (a forgotten work)

This adit lies about half way up the west side of the valley known as Nant y Maes or Cwm Bryn Moel, and is well hidden by vegetation. When I discovered the adit in 2004, the entrance was nearly completely blocked, the water inside being within 4 inches of the roof, making it quite inaccessible. With the help of my sister Rhian, I cleared enough of the rubble from the entrance to reduce the water level by several feet.

At 07.30 in the morning on the 1st of May 2004, I gained access to what I believe to be the most fascinating of all the workings encountered at Dylife.

154

Even with our drainage effort, the water in the tunnel is still over waist-deep, and the tunnel measures about 50 fathoms in a straight line from the entrance to the end. Once inside, there is a branching of the

Nant y Maes. The entrance as we found it, before enlarging and draining the tunnel

tunnel to the left, which comes very shortly to a small chamber containing a winze. I plumbed this winze and recorded a depth of 5 fathoms. Once back in the main tunnel, a fairly extensive maze of passageways unfolds, with decaying artefacts scattered throughout. The main work seems to have centred on a second winze, in a passage to the right of the main tunnel, about half way into the workings. This winze is inclined, east / west and was plumbed to a depth of 7 fathoms, or 42 feet. There are what look like the remains of a wooden vessel, with some sort of cast iron hinge mechanism for hauling the ore at the winze collar. (There are several of these vessels throughout the workings, in various stages of decay.) Also, the remains of a windlass can be seen lying on the false wooden floor that covers the top of the winze, and, nearby, a badly deteriorated shovel lies against a pile of rock, whilst on the opposite side of the winze, several chisels can be seen. The best find was yet to come. Back in the main passageway, half submerged and looking almost discarded, lay a winze kibble, intact with rope.

Bringing the Kibble out to daylight for the first time in over 120 years

I removed this and restored it, before giving it to Llywernog Mining Museum, to save it from damage, deterioration or removal to a private collection. The water in this part of the work is about knee-deep.

These workings are of utmost interest, as they have not been mentioned in any previous writings on Dylife, including Prof. O. T. Jones, *Geological Report* of 1922. Neither is it visible on any of the old maps. The find is also significant as it represents the only work east of St David's Church to amount to more than a trial. I believe these workings to be on a narrow lode that, interestingly, runs north-south, maybe branching out of the Llechwedd Ddu lode. Outside the adit there is evidence of open workings on another lode, running in the same direction and measuring about 3 feet wide at the surface.

Little is known about this work, other than it dates from the mid 1800s and was worked under the name Dylife Consols. After some years of idleness, it was reopened and 14 tons of ore were returned in 1885. It was quite eerie, being the first person there in over 100 years; apart from the obvious decay, it was as if the miners had not long left, and I can only say that this left me feeling privileged, if not a little humbled, by the achievements of the men

Nant y Maes. Remains of a windlass over the winze

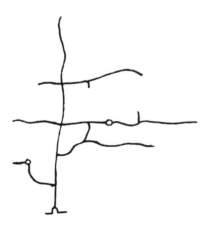

Nant y Maes (the circles denote winzes)

who had worked here long before the advent of electricity and many of the luxuries we take for granted today.

Trial 4 – Cwm Bryn Moel

The crumbling entrance to this level emerges close to the stream on the west side of the valley known as Cwm Bryn Moel and is well hidden behind a tree. Under the name of East Dyfngwm Brynmoel, it was driven by the Dyfngwm company in about 1850, before being abandoned, and it was worked again, in the 1860s, by Dylife Consols. The tunnel has been driven a total distance of 51 fathoms in a westerly direction, in an attempt to find the Esgairgaled lode, but with no success. Inside, the tunnel branches off north for a distance of 30 fathoms and runs into barren ground.

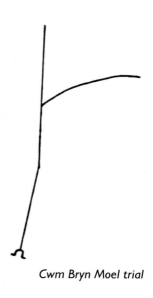

Cwm Bryn Moel trial

Nowadays, the tunnel is flooded with about 3 ft of water, before becoming dry at the point of the fork in the tunnel. There are several old iron chisels within.

Pencerrig Deep Adit

This adit commences a stone's throw from Esgairgaled shaft and is probably quite old. A level has been driven for approximately 10 fathoms, to where it cuts the Esgairgaled lode. The tunnel then turns due east and follows the lode for 153 fathoms. The lode was very hard and consisted of shattered rocks and breccia,

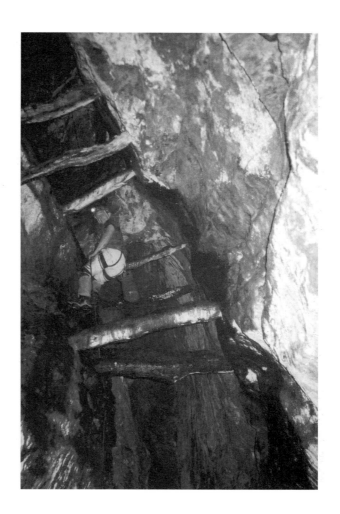

Abseiling the stopes above Pencerrig deep adit. Note the timber braces

firmly cemented together with quartz. There are four flooded winzes within, the first of which contains a wooden rising main (outside diameter 10-inches), which is probably of great antiquity, I plumbed this winze to a depth of approximately 6 fathoms, and, interestingly, the next winze, a short distance down the passage,

Pencerrig Deep Adit. The central groove along the tunnel indicates the use of wheelbarrows

plumbed the same, so it would be reasonable to assume that they both connect with the same tunnel below. Further down the passage, another winze plumbed to a depth of 14fms and had remains of a large windlass lying nearby. I had the feeling that this was where most of the later work done here had been centred. The last winze to be encountered plumbed to a depth of 7fms. With

Pencerrig Deep Adit. A windlass lies by a flooded winze

care, in 2004, the winzes could be passed by means of wooden planking, remnants of the false floors that surrounded these winzes. Above the winzes there is a fair amount of stoping, right up to the shallow adit above, although, interestingly, no stoping has been commenced east of the last winze. A central groove running along the floor of the tunnel beyond the winzes can probably be attributed to the use of wheelbarrows. This tunnel is still dry and can be explored, although, unfortunately, a substantial fall of rock has blocked access to the winzes and beyond, and, therefore, access to the best part of the work can only be achieved by abseiling down from the shallow adit above. A tip to anyone using SRT, or indeed a wire ladder: I found the natural line the rope takes is very close to several of the beams bracing the stope, making it quite easy to bang your head on it on the way out, if you're spending too much time concentrating on what your feet are doing; also, at least half of the ascent is under a small but steady stream of water that issues from somewhere above.

Pencerrig Shallow Adit

This level is situated half way up Banc Rhydwen and almost opposite Bradford Shaft. A cross cut has been driven for 20fms up to the lode and a level has been driven from there for approx 40 fathoms, on the course of the lode up to the fault. There is a lot of stopeing at the end of the tunnel, right up to the surface, where the floor of opencast workings is visible above. There is also a winze that connects with the stopes of the deep adit 60 ft

Pencerrig Shallow Adit. Mat and Al set up the ropes. We ran the rope the full length of the tunnel as there were no anchor points inside

Looking south west from Pencerrig shallow adit. Ancient workings on the Esgairgaled lode off centre, with the workings on the junction of lodes far left.

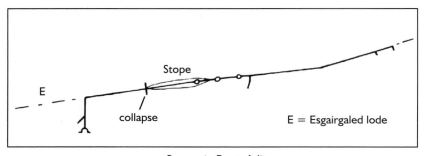

Pencerrig Deep Adit

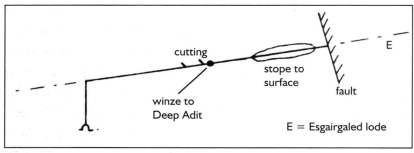

Pencerrig Shallow Adit

below. The ground around this winze is fairly unstable and should be treated with extreme caution. The entrance to these workings is flooded to about a foot and a half deep, although the tunnel quickly becomes dry where it cuts the lode. It is also interesting to note that, in the shallow adit, the lode has not been pursued beyond the fault, which, in likelihood, cut the Llechwedd Ddu lode out as well, as very little ore has been obtained east of Bradford Shaft. These workings are the eastern most on the Esgairgaled lode. O. T. Jones records: 'A few yards north of the steep path called Llwybr y Ceirw, three quarters of a mile north east of Dylife, the precipice is scored by a deep straight and narrow groove which is conspicuous from a great distance. As it is improbable that such a powerful fracture as the lode proves to be near Dylife should die away in a short distance and this groove, which is almost exactly in the line of the Esgairgaled lode, is the only break or line of weakness in the precipice, there is little doubt that it marks the position of the lode.'

Esgairgaled Shaft

Situated in the Engine Dingle, this shaft is now inaccessible due to flooding, although there are several interesting facts to relate. This shaft was the first to be sunk in Dylife, and was at work as early as 1720. The shaft has been sunk vertically to a depth of about 40 fathoms, about 15 yards north of the Esgairgaled lode, where the lode is about 18 yards wide and very hard. Levels were driven to the east and west of the shaft. The upper levels yielded a worthwhile amount of lead, although the bottom levels yielded more zinc. 150 yards along the eastern levels, the lode was cut out by the same fault encountered in the Pencerrig workings. There is an abundance of bits of lead and quartz in this valley, in the stream; according to David Bick, at one time, huge waste dumps from the works filled this little valley, although they have long since been removed. It would be very interesting to see a picture of the valley and indeed the rest of the immediate area before any mining activities took place, as it must have been a very different landscape; for example, the whole area by the phone box must be made up largely from mine waste.

Bradford Shaft

Sunk to a depth of approximately 150 fathoms this shaft is now inaccessible; over the years, it has been filled, by the Council, with a large amount of stone and old cars.

Shaft on South Lode

Inaccessible, due to being filled with stone, rubbish and old cars.

Footway Shaft

Dating from the 1820s, this footway shaft gives access to the Llechwedd Ddu lode. The entrance has remained blocked for the last twenty years or so, due to the deterioration of the shaft lining. In October 2002, I cleared enough of the blockage to allow relatively comfortable access. Once inside, explorers will quickly find themselves chest-deep in water (ie. approx 4½ ft), in a narrow tunnel that was driven south for about 8 fathoms, before entering a small chamber containing a winze sunk on the lode. There are remains of a wooden walkway on the left hand side of the chamber crossing the winze, although it is far too badly deteriorated to be used. I chose to swim across the gap, and soon began to regret the decision; on the far side of the chamber, the tunnel continued for about 2 fathoms before bearing east and finishing in a stope.

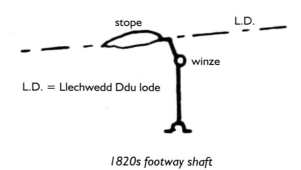

1820s footway shaft

Footway shaft on the Llechwedd Ddu lode

A substantial collapse at the end of the stope corresponds with sunken ground on the surface above. In recent years there have been several large collapses on this section of the Llechwedd Ddu lode, leaving a series of deep hollows on the surface.

Llechwedd Ddu Engine Shaft

Inaccessible due to flooding, the uppermost portion of 600 ft of pump rods makes an interesting feature. The stumps of the four massive timbers that made up the head frame can still be seen at the shaft collar, whilst on the south side of the shaft, the initials HT and WW can be seen carved into the rock. I'm afraid I can offer no explanation as to their origin, other than to say that they are both of the same period and probably quite old.

Llechwedd Ddu Engine Shaft with the remains of the Martha Wheel Drawing House in the middle distance

Gwaith Gwyn Adit

This adit is located near the Llechwedd Ddu engine shaft and opposite the Great Dylife adit. A crosscut has been driven for approx 20 fathoms up to the Esgairgaled lode, where much stopeing has been carried out, probably up to the surface. The tunnel then bears north-east for 4 fathoms, where a winze has been sunk to quite a depth, connecting with the Llechwedd Ddu lode at the 25 fathom level. Nowadays, this adit is definitely one to avoid; the tunnel is full of river silt almost to the roof and so necessitates a tight crawl. The stope to the surface has been back-filled with a lot of stone, with rubbish at the surface, all of which rest on timbers in the adit level, which will ultimately collapse. There is standing room at the end of the tunnel, but the winze

*Gwaith Gwyn. Above, the tunnel is largely silted up by the stream.
Below, the tunnel where it intersects the Esgairgaled lode*

is full of silt. I have my doubts as to the amount of fresh air in this work; there is certainly a lot of rotting vegetation washed in by the river. It is interesting to note that the name Gwaith Gwyn, meaning White Works, is probably appropriate, owing to the high amount of quartz in the vein material in this part of the lode.

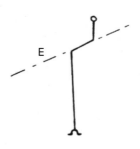

Gwaith Gwyn adit

Great Dylife Adit

The impressive entrance to this adit emerges just behind the Llechwedd Ddu engine shaft and has a cavernous appearance. The level measures 283 fathoms from the mouth to the Dylife / Dyfngwm lode, and 66 fathoms to Alfred's shaft on the new lode. Where the level meets the Dylife / Dyfngwm lode, the tunnel branches east to Old Engine shaft, and west to meet Boundary shaft, approx 200 ft below the surface. Will Richards relates how there is much stopeing above the adit level, where the ore was very bunchy up to the surface. Nowadays, the adit is only accessible up to Alfred's shaft, where it becomes completely run in due to the collapse of the shaft above. In 2003, I attempted to clear some of the blockage, to see if we could get round it. Using a system of sledges to move the waste, a friend and I spent two days in there, but it proved too much; there must be several hundred tons of mud and water jammed in the shaft, and soon after a quantity was removed, with a deep rumbling noise, more slid down from above; it had the consistency of ready mix concrete, and despite our enthusiasm, progress was slow. On the second day, work was

The Great Dylife Adit. Operating the points on the tramline for the first time in over 100 years

The Great Dylife adit

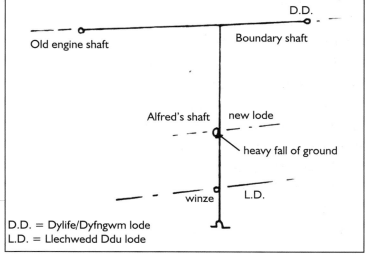

D.D.

Old engine shaft

Boundary shaft

Alfred's shaft   new lode

heavy fall of ground

winze   L.D.

D.D. = Dylife/Dyfngwm lode
L.D. = Llechwedd Ddu lode

abandoned, on the grounds of health and safety.

Just inside the adit, a flooded winze on the Llechwedd Ddu lode is visible on the left hand side; the metal support that takes the level across the lode is also visible, when the water is low. Further in, the tunnel becomes flooded, although it is not more than 2 ft deep in the worst of places, becoming dry again about 10 fathoms before it meets Alfred's shaft. (The water in this tunnel can fluctuate by several feet, depending on the time of year.) About half way between Alfred's shaft and the entrance to the adit, an iron handle can be seen sticking out of the mud on the right hand side of the tunnel. In 2003, I managed to divert enough of the water flowing through the adit to one side, to enable me to dig around this handle. As expected, upon excavation, this turned out to be what I believe operated a points system on the tramway, and it also corresponds with a widening of the tunnel nearby, maybe providing a place to allow full trams on their way out to avoid empty trams on their way in. Interestingly, although the tramway has long since been removed, straddling the points, two sleepers survived, at approximately 3ft centres. Further excavation is needed, to determine if more sleepers are in place under the mud.

Alfred's Shaft

This was the last shaft to be sunk in Dylife and dates from 1879. Its collapse in the late 1920s blocked the Dylife adit and, these days, the top of the shaft forms a deep pond on the hillside above the Llechwedd Ddu engine shaft. The shaft was sunk on a new lode, which is one of two lodes that run east to west between the Dylife / Dyfngwm lode and the Llechwedd Ddu lode; one dips north and the one that has been exploited dips south. Although only the south lode is visible in the Dylife adit, both lodes are several feet wide and filled with breccia, veined with coarsely crystallized quartz. Both lodes are exposed on the hillside south of Rydyporthmyn and 400 yards west of St David's Church. The shaft is sunk on a rich pipe of galena to a depth of 15 fathoms below the Dylife adit, and levels were driven east and west. A fair amount of lead was obtained above the adit, but the lode went very poor in the bottom level and the work was not prosecuted further, for this reason, for many years.

Trial on the Llechwedd Ddu lode. The water here is almost waist deep

Trial on the Llechwedd Ddu lode

I found this adit one day as I was walking to Level Goch. It lies in a small valley, 80 yards east of the aforementioned. Its entrance was completely covered with many years of vegetation; its presence was only given away by a small tip, and some marshy ground below the entrance. Inside, the tunnel is thigh-deep in water and stretches south for about 5 fathoms; 2 metres into the work, another tunnel branches west for 3 fathoms. Year of working is unknown, although its proximity to Level Goch could mean that it is quite old.

Level Goch

This adit emerges on the south side of the river Twymyn, and its entrance is almost completely blocked. This work is of specific interest as it is on the junction of the Esgairgaled and Llechwedd Ddu lodes and dates back a long way. I believe it was being described as an old work by the mid 1800s.

A level has been driven south for about 20 fathoms, to where it meets the lode; at this point it is stoped out to the surface and is a sight worth seeing, whether from below or above. Once inside, a tunnel branches off to the west, although it comes to nothing before returning to a central chamber in the main tunnel. All these levels are flooded to chest-deep and the water is cold. Where the adit meets the stope, the remains of a working platform is visible, and a short length

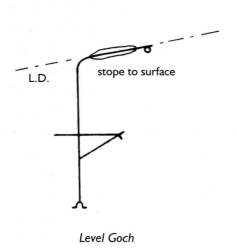

Level Goch

Junction of lodes. Large tips from the stope to daylight. Level Goch can be seen emerging at the bottom of the picture to the left of the waterfall

of wire cable lies nearby; at the end of the stope, a winze has been sunk on the lode, and a plumb-line recorded a depth of only 5 feet. The shallow height of the roof above the winze and the position of some partly buried timbers suggest that the original floor level is probably at least 6 feet or so below the present floor level. At the point where you step down through a hole in the rock to adit level, I heard the sound of running water under the rubble, and it sounded deep, I wouldn't be surprised if parts of the present floor are held up on old working platforms; the workings here certainly extend to quite a depth. The stope where it meets the surface is unfenced and should be approached with extreme caution.

I gained access to this work from above, which seemed easier at the time and preferable to a tight, muddy crawl under all that

Abseiling the stope to daylight
at the junction of lodes

Level Goch. Above, remains of a working platform where the adit meets the lode. Below, heavy iron staining above the winze at the end of the stope

loose stuff above the mouth of the adit. We found a good anchor point in the form of 2 poles wedged in the ground not far from the mouth of the upper entrance, where an interesting rock arch exists. The descent was an easy one, and took us about 40ft down to the tunnel below. On the way back out, after negotiating a bit of an overhang about half way up, there was plenty of time to inspect the vein that carries some good quartz crystals. (In the winter, a steady fall of water from above will be encountered that is difficult to avoid).

It is quite likely that this work started off in the form of an upper adit, where the lode outcropped, and that the lower adit was driven later. The isolation of this work from any roads or tracks has certainly saved it from being filled with rubbish over the years.

Boundary Shaft

Originally sunk in 1860 and eventually reaching a total depth of 167 fathoms or 1002 feet, this shaft is the deepest in mid Wales. Above the shaft, the foundations for the Cornish pumping engine can be made out and, nearby, the large, cast iron gudgeon that supported the balance bob lies at rest, whilst two large holding-down bolts stand almost as if they are guarding the gaping abyss. Close by is a heap of cinders from the two ten-ton boilers. Unfortunately, I could find no evidence of the exact position of the horse whim that was later replaced by a length of steel cable from the old engine shaft. In 2004, with my heart in my mouth, I descended the shaft as far as I could. Going over the edge, I noticed that ferns and adder's tongue were just a few of the plants that had managed to colonize the shaft collar, although this was only for the first 4 feet or so; after that the grey rock was barren and devoid of any life.

To my dismay, 135ft down, I discovered that the shaft is blocked with farm rubbish, the uppermost portion of the pump pipes are visible sticking up through the mess, whilst the large wooden pump rods that would have been connected to the beam engine extend upwards from the blockage for at least 60 feet, and make the abseil down somewhat of a daunting task. About 70 feet down, a band of quartz 6 inches wide runs around the shaft wall, and 20 feet or so below this, a ledge cut out of opposite sides of the shaft is sure to indicate the position of a large beam. Due to the waste in the shaft, I was unable to reach the adit level. It seems, therefore, that the great Dylife crosscut and the workings under Pen Dylife are blocked at every point of entry. It is perhaps fitting that the workings are sealed, for there are a lot of souls down there and it is probably best if they are left in peace.

The massive iron gudgeon – Boundary shaft

Boundary shaft – above the rubbish, the rising main is just about visible on the far side of the shaft. Below, looking back up along the pump rod timbers

Dylife Old Engine Shaft

Sadly, this shaft is inaccessible, due to it having been filled with farm rubbish. I have spent many hours walking the area in search of the position of the wheel pit that housed the pumping wheel for this shaft, but it still eludes me. Will Richards says that this is the shaft down which the blacksmith threw his wife and children in 1725.

A partially-covered opencut, not far from Old Engine Shaft

Dyfngwm

The name Dyfngwm in English translates to Deep Valley and it is exactly that. The workings total about 9 adits and 2 shafts, together with an open cut, which exploit the Dyfngwm lode on the north side of this valley. The workings here being in such a remote location, many of the features both above and below ground remain intact. As with Dylife, I have dealt with the workings from east to west, so they can be visited on a walk, limiting the need to cover the same ground twice and allowing more time to ponder and explore. The position of these workings are marked on the map on page 99.

Old Work on the Dylife/Dyfngwm lode

This old adit is about 150 yards south-east of Boundary shaft. The entrance was completely blocked, when we discovered it in 2003. Upon clearing some of the stone and wood, we discovered that a crosscut has been driven north for a distance of about 20 fathoms up to the lode, where a winze has been sunk. A tunnel had then been driven on the lode, in an easterly direction, for a fair distance. The whole of this work is flooded to waist-deep with water.

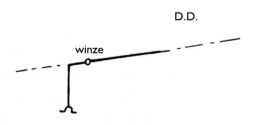

Old work on the Dylife/Dyfngwm lode

Dyfngwm Engine Shaft

This is situated on the top of the hill and is about 100 yards south-west of Boundary shaft, to the right of the cart track that descends toward the Clywedog valley. The workings here are on the outcrop of the Dyfngwm lode and are of great antiquity. On the hillside above there is much evidence of ancient activities.

Originally, drawing was achieved by the use of a horse whim (the circle is still visible today) whilst pumping was undoubtedly achieved from a wheel in the Clywedog valley, far below. A vertical scar in the rock face above the deep adit is sure to mark the course of the flatrods.

The engine shaft is connected to the east and the west with opencut workings that extend in both directions for quite a way and, probably, to a considerable depth, although, sadly, they are now either filled with stone from the tips, or are full of dead sheep and farm waste. These workings are unfenced and, in certain places, a considerable drop poses a threat to anyone who may stray from the path on a misty day, as does a small shaft midway and 20 yards south of the filled open workings. In the gulley below this shaft, a blocked adit has surely been driven under, although I did not excavate as it certainly is intersected by the shaft that is full of rubbish.

By the 1800s, these workings had become exhausted, and the main activity would have centred on the Deep adit driven from the south. About 100 yards south of the engine shaft and above the site of the 1930's incline winch, an early adit is visible and, although it is completely blocked, it almost certainly connects with the workings above.

Dyfngwm Deep Adit

The first thing that is noticeable about this adit is the remains of a shed built over the entrance with sleepers, a post on the left hand side still having a hinge that would have held the door. This shed can probably be attributed to Hirnant Minerals and dated to 1931. I cleared a little of the stone from the mouth of the adit in 1993, to let some of the water drain, but the water today is about 4 feet deep, getting shallower before becoming dry shortly before it cuts the lode. I'm not sure when this adit was driven but it was definitely in existence in 1812, having been driven under the old and exhausted workings above; we know it was widened to provide extra room for the flatrods in 1855. As would be expected, the tunnel is of a good size and measures approx 100 fathoms,

Dyfngwm Main Adit. Clearing the entrance, Easter 1993

Dyfngwm Main Adit. A large pillar of rock supports the roof of the large chamber around the main shaft

from the entrance to the Dyfngwm lode. (About half way along the adit, a stope has been commenced on another lode.) The adit, where it meets the Dyfngwm lode, terminates in a large chamber that, in the 1860s, would have contained two angle bobs (one inverted for twin pumps), and a capstan.

To the right of the chamber, a section of the lode has been left in the form of a pillar to support the ceiling, and also a tunnel has been driven east on the lode but, after 23 fathoms, this becomes run in due to a heavy fall of ground from above, where old tram rails can be seen. These were used as planking, to support waste dropped down from stopes above. In this level and in the main adit, a wooden gutter to take the water out is visible.

I did not realise myself, until I had explored the tunnel below,

Dyfngwm Main Shaft

that this entire tunnel has a false floor; i.e. just a few old beams and tram rails covered with a layer of rock separate the explorer from the stopes below. As there is not much to see in this end of the mine, it is best avoided altogether.

A similar tunnel has been driven west from the chamber, although, after only a few fathoms, a large section of the floor has collapsed into the stope below, which is quite large and extends in places down about 70ft, before backing onto the main shaft. Beyond this collapse, the tunnel continues at adit level, but as yet remains unexplored. Nearby, a fine ore shoot connects with workings above, and, interestingly, if you hold your face to it, a draft can be felt, certainly proving good ventilation between the adit level and the surface workings that surround the engine shaft far above. A lot of farm rubbish is also visible, having been

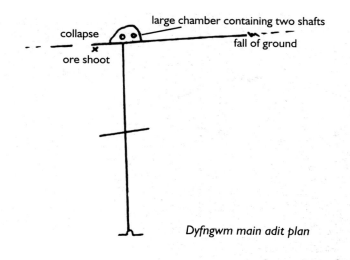

Dyfngwm main adit plan

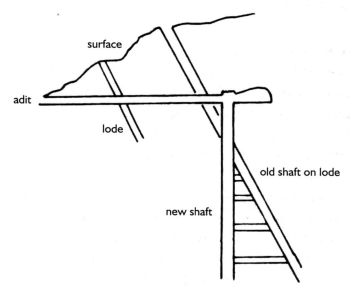

Section of Dyfngwm main shaft, 1935 (based on a sketch by Will Richards)

Dyfngwm Deep Adit. Above, eastern tunnel on the lode.
Below, this fine example of an ore shoot brought ore down from a level above

Dyfngwm Deep Adit. Western tunnel on the lode

thrown down from above. At this point, you are several hundred feet under the top of the mountain. Inside the chamber I found a small winze and the main shaft. The small winze is open at the top and sunk for about 10 fathoms down to a level driven east on the lode; this level extends for a fair distance before coming to an end. The ground has been stoped out up to the floor above, where the supporting timbers are quite visible, making the danger far more apparent. It is quite possible that the floor of this 10-fathom level has been created in a similar way, so great care must be taken. The main shaft, also open and displaying a dangerous void, is not far away and is in quite a good state. Water is visible about eighty feet down, and it seems that all the ladders except the top one are still intact. Above the main shaft, a shaft can be seen leading upwards, crossed by several metal I-section beams that can probably be attributed to the Hirnant Minerals era.

All in all, you get the impression of much work having been done here, and it is well worth taking a moment to switch off your headlight. If you listen hard enough, it is almost possible to hear the clatter of the trams, and the clink of tools against rock, but only ghost horses pull the trams of ore out to the daylight now.

Trial 1 on Dylife lode

This trial is between the Dyfngwm main adit and the Cyfartha works and may date back to 1848, being one of Captain Davies's trials. The entrance is almost completely blocked, although its position is marked by a large waste tip. A bit of a squeeze is required to gain access to the adit, and the rock above is none to stable. Once inside, a slightly meandering tunnel of a good size has been driven north for a distance of 32 fathoms. Three fathoms from the end of the tunnel there is a cutting to the left, and, to the right, a tunnel has been driven east for several fathoms but does not come to much.

The trial, I think, cuts the Dylife lode, but no ore was found. Today, the main passageway is waist-deep in water, which gradually becomes shallower the further in you get, being about a foot deep at the junction of the passageways. There are no winzes or stopes within.

Trial 1 on Dylife lode

Trial 2 on Dylife lode

Situated close to the top of the slope on the north side of the valley and not far from Llwybr Asynod, a trial has been made on the Dylife lode. This adit can also probably be attributed to Captain Edward Davies, and dates from around 1848–1850. The adit has been driven north for about 3 fathoms but no lead was found. The adit is still quite accessible, although there is not much to see inside, except for a hole to daylight, mid way along the tunnel. However, a fantastic view of the sett is gained from the entrance. To the west, Llwybr Asynod descends toward Castle Rock; to the east, the Afon Clywedog, far below, winds its way down toward the foundations of the Hirnant Minerals dressing plant.

Cyfartha Shallow adit

This adit is the upper of two that are driven to the Dyfngwm lode. This mine is very old, and outside the entrance are vestiges of a wheel pit that once contained a small, iron waterwheel for pumping; one of the flatrods still lies intact under the rubble that largely blocks the entrance, and there is another inside, at the shaft collar.

The adit has been driven north for 14 fathoms, to a chamber containing a shaft that connects with the deep adit about 70ft below. At the top of the shaft, a pit cut out of the rock and measuring approx 10ft x 6ft x10ft deep contains substantial remains of the angle bob, whilst part of the pump is also visible; it has somehow become removed and is attached to a chain, that itself is attached to a beam that braces the bottom of a stope above the chamber. Inside the entrance to the adit, on the left hand side,

Cyfarthfa Shallow Adit. The large chamber, with a flatrod protruding from the balance pit on the left, and the shaft just beyond

are the wood and iron supports that most likely carried a roller to support the flatrods. Also, a few sleepers in the mud mark the course of a tramway, although this adit was probably chiefly used for pumping; the shallow adit below being used for extraction.

These supports carried a roller for the flatrods

Cyfartha Shallow Adit. Substantial remains of the bob, a large part of which dangles over the edge of the shaft down to the deep adit below

Cyfartha Deep adit

This adit has been driven from the river for a distance of 40 fathoms, to where it meets the shaft, It is a tunnel of very generous proportions, certainly large enough to admit horses, and I would go so far as to say that it is probably one of the widest in the area, almost on the same scale as the great Dylife crosscut. Unfortunately, a waste tip above the entrance has slipped, completely blocking the entrance, so that the only way to get in is by abseiling down from the shallow adit, to which it is connected by a shaft for pumping. The adit to this point is waist-deep in water; beneath the water the tramway is still completely intact. Along this adit, several tunnels lead off to the east and west but come to nothing. Near to the shaft

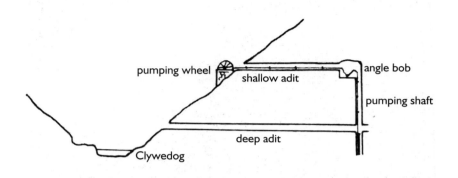

Cyfartha – section

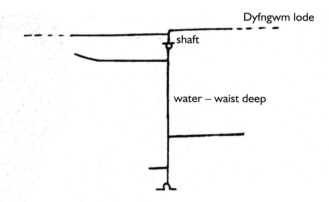

Cyfartha deep adit – plan

Cyfartha Deep Adit. This unusually wide tunnel is flooded to waist deep and still contains a tramway. Below, a small waterwheel for driving a ventilation fan

are the remains of a small waterwheel, used for driving a ventilation fan. It used to be intact and I understand it was broken, many years ago, by someone abseiling down the shaft from above, who accidentally landed on it... The boards covering the shaft (which I plumbed to a depth of about 15 fathoms), are in reasonable shape, and the remains of a windlass are visible under the water, whilst the pump and rod are also intact, if a little bent. Beyond the shaft, a dry tunnel bears east and another tunnel, driven on the course of the lode, bears west for a considerable distance. This tunnel becomes increasingly flooded, until the water is within a couple of inches of the roof, and it was at this point that we turned back. The end of this tunnel cannot be a great distance away from the level driven east from the Castle Rock area. This mine was an old work when it was reopened by the Dyfngwm Company in 1848. Little else is known other than that it was active again in 1861, under the direction of Captain Edward Davies.

Cyfartha Deep Adit. A chamber contains a shaft and pump, with tunnels heading east and west on the lode behind

Inside the Roman level

The Cutting and the Roman level

This small cutting is 50 yards west of the Cyfartha works. Here, an opencast work has been carried out on a small lode running north–south that branches out of the Dyfngwm lode. In 1931, Hirnant Minerals had set a few men to work in this cutting, and any ore raised would have been taken to their dressing plant further down the valley, although Will Richards records that no ore was taken. Great care must be taken if approaching this work along the Dyfngwm leat, as a section of the leat is missing, having been mined out, and there is no warning of the 25ft drop that the unsuspecting walker may happen upon.

Just inside the entrance of the cutting, on the left-hand side, a small level has been driven in a north westerly direction for 26 fathoms, a branch tunnel inside leads to a winze about a fathom and a half deep. Will Richards attributed this level to the Romans and, whilst it is not a coffin level, it is quite narrow and certainly very old. It is said that an old wheelbarrow was found within but did not survive the removal. Whilst the entrance for a short distance may be Roman, the winze and far end of the tunnel are post-1600s, as there is evidence of powder holes. The tunnel is very dry and quite possible to explore, although much water issues down from the cutting at the entrance.

Dyfngwm – Trial 3

I discovered this adit on the 7th of January 2005 quite by chance, whilst the rest of the book was in the hands of the publishers undergoing the first edit, so it is lucky that this find made it to print. The adit is situated on the hillside above the alleged Roman level and the cutting. It emerges onto the ancient track, Llwybr Asynod.

The level, which is well-hidden, has been driven north for approximately four fathoms to try the Dyfngwm lode, but no work has been undertaken. The tunnel has a very square entrance, and is knee-deep in water. As regards a date, I can only say it probably predates the 1800s.

Inside the trial on the Dyfngwm lode. Taken from Trial Adit No. 3.
Below: 1) Trial No. 1 adit on the Dylife lode; 2) Trial adit No. 2 on the Dylife
lode; 3) Dyfngwm leat; 4) Tramway to cutting; 5) Tramway from Cyfartha
deep adit

Castle Rock

At the westernmost end of the Dyfngwm sett, Castle Rock towers out of the ravine above the infant Afon Clywedog, some 120ft below.

Castle Rock is actually part of the Esgairgaled lode and forms part of what O. T. Jones called 'The finest natural exposure of a lode in the country.' On the south side of the stream, the base of the rock has been tried by a small level, 1 fathom in length, whilst, above the pool, a rib of lead ore is visible. On the opposite bank, a flooded shaft and a level are visible. The workings here were probably the first in the valley, and were in being a long time before ore was discovered at Dyfngwm. The level, which is of a good size, follows the lode east for 7 fathoms, with a small stope about 4 fathoms along, there are no winzes within, and the work is flooded to about 3 feet deep. I imagine that some lead was obtained above the entrance to the adit, judging from excavations visible on the lode.

Close to the river are the remains of a wheel pit that housed a pumping wheel; the pit measures approx 15ft x 6ft. On the base of Castle Rock, on the opposite bank, are three distinctive square holes. I wonder if these held timbers, which perhaps once formed part of a dam on the Clywedog, to provide water for the pumping wheel.

Near the top of the rocky hillside above the arch for the Dyfngwm leat, a hollow conceals what is almost certainly the blocked entrance to a short level, whilst above, ancient opencut workings are visible, although largely filled with debris of the years. Beyond, near a prominent rocky outcrop, a series of heaps and hollows is visible that certainly relate to ancient times, although they defy my powers of interpretation.

Above Castle Rock, the river channel has been excavated for over three hundred yards along the hanging wall of the lode, while the south slope of the ravine is formed by a towering wall-like mass, which is the lode itself, and behind this is the depression that marks the footwall. The geology here is fascinating and, if the sun is out, I strongly recommend a walk along the river here, up as far as Nant Ddu.

It is about 100 yards up this river channel that 2 iron pins in the river bed mark the beginning of the Dyfngwm leat, being vestiges of the sluice system that drew water off to convey via the leat to the pumping and crushing wheels, over half a mile down the valley. Opposite Castle Rock, the leat passes through the lode by means of a short tunnel.

Downstream from the pumping wheel pit, a path ascends the steep side of the valley and emerges just behind the uppermost trial on the Dylife lode. This path is known as Llywbr Asynod (Asses' path), and is the route the asses took, many years ago, to carry the lead out of the valley.

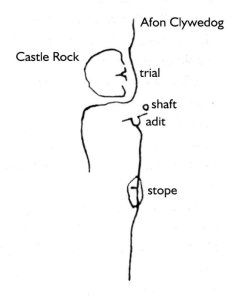

The Castle Rock area

Glossary

Adit
A level driven into the mountain to facilitate access and drainage

Blende
Zinc ore, typical composition, 67% zinc, 33% sulphur

Buddle
A device for separating finely crushed ore from the gangue, usually consists of rotating brushes powered by a waterwheel

Crosscut
A level or adit driven in order to cut a lode or occasionally a tunnel driven to connect one work with another i.e. Llechwedd Ddu with Gwaith Gwyn

Drawing Machine
This is the old term for a winding engine

Dressing
The process of separating the ore from the waste material i.e. quartz and rock

Engine Shaft
A shaft fitted with pumping gear

Fathom
The standard unit of measurement for mining purposes, 1 fathom is equal to 6 feet

Firesetting
Fires lit underground to heat and thus loosen the rock

Flatrods
Lengths of iron bar, or sometimes wood, about 20ft in length. These were connected to the waterwheel and supported on rollers, for the purpose of transmitting power

Galena
Lead ore, typical composition 86% lead, 14% sulphur

Gangue
The ore matrix, comprising fragments of rock cemented together with quartz, calcite etc

Horse Whim
A large drum made of wood, around which rope could be wound and powered by horses, this device was used for winding

Jigs
Were used to separate ore by agitating a sieve in a tank of water by means of a long pole. The lead ore would sink to the mesh bottom of the sieve and the zinc just above it, the top layer was waste and was removed with a scraper

Kibble

Effectively, a kibble was a bucket made of iron or wood, used to bring ore to the surface. There are two sizes of kibble, the larger being a shaft kibble, raised by horse whim or waterwheel. The smaller, a winze kibble, was raised by windlass

Launder

A trough usually made of wood, for the purpose of conveying water from one place to another

Lode

Mineralised ground, in the form of near vertical veins containing ore in conjunction with material of no value, i.e. quartz, rock etc

Opencut

An excavation, often narrow and deep, on the course of a lode

Potter's Ore

A high quality ore, used as a glaze in pottery making

Rise

A stope commenced upwards from the back of a level

Stope

Cavities in a mine created by the removal of ore, these can range in size from quite small to massive. A stope I encountered at nearby Rhoswydol mines could have accomodated four or five double-decker buses

Tribute

This was ground let to different miners at prearranged prices per ton of ore ready for sale

Windlass

A device used for winding ore, comprising of a round timber that rope could be wound around with a handle at each end, mounted on a frame over the shaft or winze

Winze

An underground shaft excavated downwards for the purpose of connecting levels, aiding ventilation and dividing tributes

BIBLIOGRAPHY

1. *Dylife*, 1975, new edition 1985, David Bick
2. *The Old Metal Mines of Mid Wales, Parts 4 and 6*, 1977 and 1991, David Bick
3. *Lead Mining in Wales*, 1967, W.J. Lewis
4. *Memoirs of the Geological Survey*, The Mining District of North Cardiganshire and West Montgomeryshire, 1922, Professor O.T. Jones
5. *Welsh History Review*, Cobden and Bright and *The Dylife Lead Mines*, C.J. Williams
6. *Calon Blwm*, Cyril Jones
7. Notes on Dylife and Dyfngwm, the late Will Richards
8. Notes and sketches concerning Dyfngwm, the late Tommy Wilson
9. *Mining Journals* 1835–1890 (National Library of Wales)
10. Bundles of letters from Richard Cobden (National Library of Wales)
11. The Wynnstay Estate papers (Denbighshire Record Office)
12. Mine Plans (Powys and Denbighshire Record Offices)
13. *Vagabond Book*, Number 1, Don Gardner

In addition to these titles I found the internet a handy source of material.

Further Reading

Despite the growing interest in Welsh metal mines and their history, books on the subject are surprisingly few and far between and in my opinion cannot be given enough publicity. The following are books of related interest that over the years I have found to be not only easy to understand and follow, but outstanding in their own particular way;

1. *Metal Mines of North Wales – A Collection of Pictures*, C. J. Williams, 1997
2. *The Old Metal Mines of Mid Wales*, Parts 1–6, David Bick 1977–1991
3. *The Cornish Beam Engine*, D.B. Barton
4. *Steam engines and Waterwheels*, Frank Woodall, 1975
5 *Underground Wales*, Martyn Farr, 2001
6. *Lead Mining in Wales*, W.J. Lewis, 1967
7. *Waller's Description of the Mines in Cardiganshire*, David Bick, 2004
8. *Mountains and Orefields*, Jones, Walters and Frost, 2004

Visitor Centres

Llywernog Silver Lead Mine Museum, Ceredigion
01970 890620 www.silverminetours.co.uk

Dolaucothi Gold Mines, Carmarthenshire
01558 650177 www.nationaltrust.org.uk

Llechwedd Slate Caverns, Gwynedd
01766 830306 www.grouptrotter.net

Sygun Copper Mine, Snowdonia
01766 510100 www.syguncoppermine.co.uk

Minera Lead Mines, Wrexham
01978 753400 www.wrexham.gov.uk

ACKNOWLEDGEMENTS

When writing a book such as this, many people become involved along the way. It is not always possible to remember them all, and if you are one of those people and do not see your name here, I apologise.

First to thank is David Bick, who has been more than helpful and to whom I am indebted for allowing me to reproduce several items from his own book, including various quotes from the Cobden and Bright period and the sketch of the Esgairgaled area in the 1840s.

The notes of the late Tommy Wilson and Will Richards have proved deeply interesting, giving a precious insight into the history of the area.

Thanks also to the British Museum for the picture of Richard Cobden, and to the National Museum of Wales for the photo of the skull and gibbet, whilst the National Library of Wales was kind enough to allow me to reproduce the plan of 1774. Ordnance Survey permitted reproduction of the 1st and 2nd edition maps of the area. The Countryside Council for Wales allowed me to reproduce the SSSI Citation, and Ordnance Survey the accompanying map. I am also grateful to Dyfed Roberts for his help regarding mine plans, and also to Denbighshire Record Office for allowing their reproduction. Also Powys Record Office for allowing reproduction of all the 1877 plans. Thanks to the Sedgwick Museum, University of Cambridge, for permission to reproduce photographs and to Dudley Simons for all his help. Also to Dafydd Saer at Y Lolfa for his enthusiasm and creative input.

A big thank you is also due to all the people who have assisted me with underground exploration over the years, namely, Matthew Starnes, Alastair Durkin, Gareth Coggan, and James Boden. Venturing into the darkness is not everyone's idea of fun, but those who do it are of a special breed.

My thanks also go to the local people whose first-hand knowledge has been invaluable: Gwilam Wilson, Blaen Twymyn; Gwen Rees, Aberhosan; and Trevor Rowlands, Cae Penwyn. The older generation have a lot to say; if we can find the time to listen, we can learn a lot from them.

Also thanks to Nick Humphries of Staylittle Stores for the photo of Rhod Goch and the Dylife postcard, and to Trevor Wilson for lending me the pictures of his father. Sue and Daniel Ward-Banks of the Star Inn have been great and have given assistance over the years in more ways than I can remember.

Thank you to my mother for help typing the manuscript, and to my father for introducing me to the area and for the photos of the demolition of St David's Church, also to my girlfriend, Kate, for putting up with my continued absence, as weekend after weekend has been spent pottering about in the mountains.

Last, but not least, I thank my sister Rhian for her continued enthusiasm and support on all of the expeditions on which she has accompanied me, regardless of the weather.

* * *

As is so often the case with publications of this nature, due to economic factors and the specialist nature of the book, the author is called upon to pay for the initial production costs himself. Financial assistance and support was very gratefully received from Cadw under their civic initiatives (Heritage) grants scheme as well as the following friends, family and local businesses. To them I will be eternally grateful. Aneirin and Bethan Lewis and family, Bacheiddon; Mr D Rees, formerly of Cwmbiga; Alastair Durkin; Kate Rodgers; my father, sisters, Rhian and Cerian, and my grandmother, Mrs E Brown; also Tom, Betty and Arwel Griffiths, Dolbachog.

Notes

A book of this nature is never truly finished. These pages have been left blank for the reader to make their own notes should they so wish.

Titles already published

For more information
about this innovative imprint,
contact Lefi Gruffudd at
lefi@ylolfa.com
or go to www.ylolfa.com/dinas.
A Dinas catalogue
is also available.